The Choice Is *Yours*

52 Choices

for Happier Lives

Barbara Dahlgren

The Choice Is

Yours

52 Choices
for Happier Lives

REDEMPTION
PRESS

Published by Redemption Press, PO Box 427, Enumclaw, WA 98022.

Toll-Free (844) 2REDEEM (273-3336)

Redemption Press is honored to present this title in partnership with the author. The views expressed or implied in this work are those of the author. Redemption Press provides our imprint seal representing design excellence, creative content, and high-quality production.

ISBN: 978-1-68314-971-2
     978-1-68314-972-9 (ePub)
     978-1-68314-973-6 (Mobi)

Library of Congress Catalog Card Number: 2019909483

Contents

Introduction
The Choice Is Yours

L ife is full of choices. All day long we make decisions. Will we eat healthy or not? Will we exercise or not? Will we stay under the speed limit or not? Will we forgive or not? Will we gossip or not? Will we accept that Jesus loves us unconditionally or not?

Choices are important! Right choices bring peace of mind; bad choices bring distress. God does not need to zap us when we do something wrong because wrong choices bring their own consequences. When we make wrong choices, we punish ourselves. The cause-and-effect principle goes into effect. What we sow, we reap. While it's true God forgives sin, the effect of sin that comes from poor choices will remain.

Eleanor Roosevelt said, "One's philosophy is not best expressed in words. It is expressed in the choices one makes. In the long run, we shape our lives and we shape ourselves. The process never ends until we die. And the choices we make are ultimately our responsibility."[1]

From a spiritual perspective, we must never think our choices will make God love us more. Nor should we think God's love for us depends on our decisions. Nothing can separate us from the love of God (Romans 8:35–38). Many think they must change before God loves

---

[1] Eleanor Roosevelt Quotes, BrainyQuote.com, BrainyMedia Inc, 2019, https://www.brainyquote.com/quotes/eleanor_roosevelt_121041

them. Nothing could be further from the truth. Believe it or not, God loves the real us.

We might want to make some changes in our lives, but we don't have to change to earn God's love. Salvation is a gift from God. We do not earn it. We accept it. However, the Bible is full of Scriptures about changing destructive behavior and making right choices.

Some may ask, If our salvation is not dependent on earning God's love or having salvation, then why bother?

Here is one way to look at it. We all know that there is something special about parental love. Those of us with children have given them not only our love but also all kinds of instructions and advice. When they take our admonitions to heart, it pleases us. Their obedience doesn't (or shouldn't) make us love them more, but it does gratify us to know they've listened and responded to what we said. Why? Because we know their lives will be more comfortable and more productive when they heed our instructions. We are older and wiser.

Similarly, God is our loving Father. When we heed His instructions, it pleases Him. Why? Because He knows we will be happier and lead more fulfilling lives if we do what He says. Christ says, "If you know these things, blessed are you if you do them" (John 13:17). The King James translation says, "Happy are ye if ye do them." Don't we all want to be happy?

We don't need to follow a list of dos or don'ts for God to love us. He already loves us. He's forgiven us for our sins—all our sins—past, present, and future. However, if we love God, we will listen to what He says and try to implement it in our lives. He wants only the best for us. He knows what will make us happy. We think we know what will make us happy, but we don't. God knows, and God wants us to be happy.

Jesus wants us to have the more abundant life (John

10:10). Having the abundant life with Jesus Christ is not a onetime event, but a daily walk with God. God should be our guide in our Christian walk. If we listen carefully, we will hear His voice saying, "This is the way, walk in it" (Isaiah 30:21).

A small voice inside us sometimes cautions, "I probably shouldn't do this . . ." or "If I do this something bad will happen . . ." When that voice speaks, we should listen instead of saying, "But I'll do it anyway." But the choice is ours! And we need to accept responsibility for the choices we make instead of blaming others and God for them.

Not only do our good choices make a difference in our lives, but they also make a difference in the lives of those around us. Our choices become a light to others. People see them, and they glorify God (Matthew 5:16).

While it's true that bad things can happen to good people through no fault of their own, we still choose how we let those situations affect us. Will we choose to become bitter or better? We may not always have control of our lives, but we can control the choices we make in every circumstance. We choose whether we will act or react. We know we cannot control people, but we can determine not to let them control our responses or thoughts.

Perhaps that's one reason we are told to think about or meditate on "whatever is true, whatever is noble, whatever is right, whatever is pure, whatever is lovely, whatever is admirable, or whatever is praiseworthy" (Philippians 4:8). Paul goes on to say, "The things which you learned and received and heard and saw in me, these do, and the God of peace will be with you" (Philippians 4:9). Making right choices brings peace in every aspect of our lives.

The New International Version (NIV) Bible says, "Put it into practice." What a novel thought! Whatever we have learned, we are to put into practice. We've heard that practice makes perfect. I'm not sure if practice always brings perfection, but it does bring progress. The more we practice making good choices, the easier it becomes. Good choices make us and everyone around us happier.

Each year is filled with infinite possibilities. Each new day is filled with choices that can help those possibilities become reality.

Suggestions for Using This Book

This book is a compilation of a weekly blog I've done for the past five years. I've chosen to include those that garnered the most response from readers. I don't presume to know how this book can best benefit you, other than planting thoughts in your mind. However, here are a few suggestions.

Look up Scriptures. If you don't have a Bible, I suggest you buy one. I deliberately did not write out every Scripture because I think we should be reading our Bibles and not just relying on what we think it says. Plus, there is something about having to do it yourself that makes you remember it longer. You may even want to mark a specific Scripture in colored pencil or with a sticky note if you think you will want to refer to it again. While many translations are available today, I have used the New King James Version unless otherwise noted. When I referred to other translations, I listed them. Most translations will have the gist of a Scripture verse. Try not to get too hung up on semantics, but get the overview of what a passage is saying.

Some find it beneficial to concentrate on one choice a week. The practice ideas listed can be implemented daily or weekly. Others like to come up with their own ideas on how to practice a choice. If you have an idea that worked particularly well for you, I'd love to hear about it. You can contact me through my blog site: Barbara's Banter at www.barbdahlgren.com.

Many may not know that I am a humorist. I believe God created laughter and it is good. "A merry heart is good medicine" (Proverbs 17:22). So if you find something in this book you think is funny, I suggest you smile instead of taking offense. My philosophy is to take my faith, but not myself, too seriously. I think the world would be a far better place if we laughed more and criticized less.

Some have used this book as a group Bible study that meets once a week. In one year, the study is complete because there are fifty-two choices—one for each week of the year.

Whether you use this book as a tool to draw closer to God, pass it on to someone else, or throw it in the trash is up to you. After all, the choice is yours!

Choice #1
Choose to Believe in God

Scientists and Christians have one thing in common. They choose to believe what they think is right.

Many scientists want desperately to convince Christians there is no God. They come up with theories of how the world came into existence, how life began, and how humans developed into the highest life form. (Yes, I know certain humans make us doubt that last point, but you know what I mean.) However, there are holes in each theory that cannot be explained. So they choose to disregard weaknesses in their thinking and believe what they want to believe. Personally, I find it hard to believe humans evolved to the place where no two people in the billions and billions and billions—dead or alive—have the same fingerprints, exact voice pattern, or DNA, but a scientist may have difficulty believing Jesus healed the blind and lame.

Many Christians want just as desperately to convince others that God does exist. They use clever arguments, saying that without God life has no meaning, creation demands a Creator, and scientific theories change but God remains the same. However, it's hard to convince an atheist that Jesus was born to a virgin, died for our sins only to be resurrected three days later, and lives in us.

Einstein had an interesting thought on science and religion: "Science without religion is lame; religion without science is blind."[2] There might be some truth there.

Both science and Christianity require an element of faith. Likewise, in Joshua's day, the Israelites had to choose whether to follow a God they could not see or the gods of the nations around them. Joshua challenged them, "Choose . . . whom you will serve" (Joshua 24:15). Joshua made his choice. "But as for me and my house, we will serve the Lord" (Joshua 24:15).

Consider this. God doesn't need us to believe in Him. He's not some Tinkerbell relying on us whispering, "I do believe in fairies; I do believe in fairies," to extend His life. God is God. Always was and always will be! We can choose to believe in Him or not. After all, He created us with free will.

The benefits of choosing to believe in God are many. No longer will we feel alone or abandoned. Our life outlook will improve. We will live with purpose, not just flounder around trying to justify our existence. And true belief in God brings inner peace so we won't feel like we need to defend our faith, just live it.

Suggestions for practicing this choice:

- Ask God to help your unbelief when doubts arise (Mark 9:24).
- Resist the temptation to debate issues trying to convince others to see things your way. Most of us don't have the knowledge to win such a debate, although we think we do.
- Let people believe what they want to believe and don't put them down. We aren't the belief police.
- Rely on God to reveal Himself to others in His time. Be ready to support His process,

---

[2] Albert Einstein Quotes, BrainyQuote.com, BrainyMedia Inc, 2019, https://wwwbrainyquote.com/quotes/albert_einstein_161289

not inadvertently circumvent it. It's okay to give an answer for the hope that lies within you when asked, but resist the temptation to shove God in someone's face.

- Ask God to solidify your belief in Him so you can honestly say, "As for me, I will believe in God."

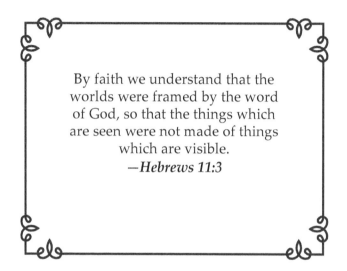

By faith we understand that the worlds were framed by the word of God, so that the things which are seen were not made of things which are visible.
—*Hebrews 11:3*

Do you have any suggestions for practicing this choice?

1. _____

2. _____

3. _____

4. _____

5. _____

Choice #2
Choose to View God as a Loving God

Many choose to view God as an all-powerful judge who is eager to plague us with disease, disaster, and disgrace when we tick Him off. A list of dos and don'ts becomes a gauge to measure their success in pleasing Him. We think if we don't live up to God's expectations, He will zap our lives with a lightning bolt to shock us into obedience. Others choose to view God as caring and kind.

How we view God can influence our actions and motives, even subconsciously. Theologian A.W. Tozer expressed it this way in his book *The Knowledge of the Holy:* "What comes into our minds when we think about God is the most important thing about us." Our image of God affects every choice we make. Tozer compared having a right concept of God to a foundation of a building. "Where it is inadequate or out of plumb, the whole structure must sooner or later collapse." [3]

Some have laid a wrong foundation when entering into a relationship with God. They become Christians just to escape eternal punishment. If we turn to God because we are afraid He will burn us in a lake of fire if we don't, it is like marrying someone just so they won't kill us. Fear is not the kind of foundation where a loving relationship can thrive. One lives in constant

[3] A. W. Tozer, The Knowledge of the Holy (New York: Harper and Brothers, 1961), 4.

fear that if God is not pleased, He will open the trap door to hell.

On the other hand, if we embrace God because He sent His only begotten Son to live among us (John 1:14), serve us (Mark 10:42–45), and freely die for us (John 3:16, John 10:18), our foundation becomes one of love, not fear. In fact, God did all these things for us because He does love us—unconditionally. He might hate what we sometimes do, but that never deters His love for us.

Consider this. God doesn't need to zap us into obedience because sin carries its own penalty. When we misbehave, we set off an automatic cause-and-effect sensor. We will reap what we sow. What goes around will eventually come around to bite us in the backside.

Although it's more convenient just to blame God for our troubles, God is not the enemy. God is love (1 John 4:8). Just because He doesn't give us what we want doesn't mean He doesn't love us. Just because He doesn't miraculously intervene every time we ask Him to doesn't mean He doesn't love us.

How we choose to view God determines our relationship with Him. Viewing God as love helps us feel loved, accepted, and wanted. God is the Father, Son, and Holy Spirit, all working together in harmony. God invites us to participate in this loving relationship and know Him intimately. Trust and confidence are built by daily walking and talking with Him. He desires to be a helper of our joy, not a policeman of our faith (2 Corinthians 1:24). As we come to know God more intimately, we realize He has only our best interests in mind. He is for us, not against us. God is love!

Suggestions for practicing this choice:

- Repeat this phrase when needed. "Everyone else may think I'm a jerk, but God loves me."
- Resist the temptation to think God is out to get you. Say this instead, "God is for me, not against me."
- Enhance your relationship with God by daily talking to Him and reading His Word—the Bible. If this seems overwhelming, start small but be consistent. Even five minutes a day is better than nothing.
- As you do this, ask God to help you see Him as a God of love.

He who does not love does not know God, for God is love.
—1 John 4:8

Do you have any suggestions for practicing this choice?

1. _____

2. _____

3. _____

4. _____

5. _____

Choice #3
Choose to Take God as He Is

Theologian A. W. Tozer said, "Much of our difficulty as seeking Christians stems from our unwillingness to take God as He is and adjust our lives accordingly. We insist upon trying to modify Him and to bring Him nearer to our own image." [4]

Academically, we want to be made into God's image (Genesis 1:26). Emotionally, we want to make God over into our image, so we tend to give Him a spiritual facelift—a nip here and a tuck there, so He can reflect us instead of us reflecting Him.

Subconsciously, we think God tends to reflect our own personalities. This can influence the choices we make. Introverts might think God is distant and not all that interested in our day-to-day lives, so they withdraw from interaction with others. Extroverts might think God is the life of the party, so they live it up. Happy people might think God wants to give everyone a big hug, so they smile, smile, smile. Angry people might think God wants to annihilate everyone, so they stay grumpy. Activists might think God is interested in social change, so they run for office. Pacifists might think God will just let everything take its course, so they remain uninvolved.

To carry it a step further, many of us think God likes what we like and hates what we hate. If we are vegetar-

---

[4] A. W. Tozer, *The Pursuit of God* (Harrisburg: Christian Publications Inc., 1948), 101.

ians, God visits the salad bar. If we sing country music, God wears a Stetson and strums a guitar. If we are rich, God lives in a mansion. If we are poor, God lives in a shack.

We even think God judges a matter the way we would judge. We think His views are our views. Of course, this makes life so much easier because the phrase "what would Jesus do" quickly morphs into "what would I do." Having preferences or opinions is fine as long as we don't think they are the standard for righteousness. For example, humans place more importance on some sins than others. That doesn't mean God feels the same way.

What we feel is not as important as what God feels. What we think is not as important as what God thinks. Our thoughts are not God's thoughts (Isaiah 55:8). Our views are not necessarily God's views, and almost assuredly our preferences are not the same as His. This may come as a shock, but God does not like what we like just because we like it. God does not hate what we hate just because we hate it. God does not react how we react just so we can justify what we do. If He did, we would not need to seek the mind of Christ and be transformed (Philippians 2:5; Romans 12:2). Therefore, we should strive to align our thinking with God's, not His to ours.

Consider this. God is God and we are not. Choose to take God as He is! After all, that's how He takes us.

Suggestions for practicing this choice:

- Abstain from judging others based on their preferences.
- Repeat this often: "God is God and I am not."
- Avoid presumptions about knowing what God thinks about certain issues unless it

can be backed up biblically. Exactly where is that passage used to reinforce that information? What does the whole passage say? Can it be cross-referenced with other Scriptures to support that view?

- Don't misinterpret Scriptures or take them out of context to back up personal views.
- Seek the mind of Christ through prayer and Bible study. A brief daily prayer might be, "Lord, help me to align my thoughts to Yours."

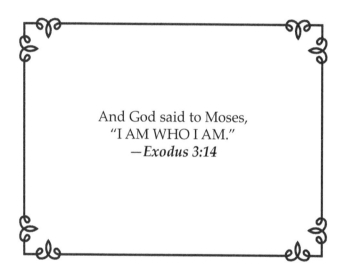

And God said to Moses,
"I AM WHO I AM."
—*Exodus 3:14*

Do you have any suggestions for practicing this choice?

1. _____

2. _____

3. _____

4. _____

5. _____

Choice #4
Choose to Know More about Jesus

Many skeptics assume they know all about Jesus Christ based on what they have heard or assumptions they've made. They might consider God a myth, superstition, or just wishful thinking—and if Jesus did walk this earth, He was probably just a kind man or perhaps a gifted teacher who could tell great stories. The more spiritual might even think Jesus was a prophet, but not the Son of God. However, even if we can't accept the Bible as inspired, it is hard to deny the existence of Jesus Christ. There are too many eyewitnesses.

Four such eyewitnesses were Matthew, Mark, Luke, and John. They endeavored to give accurate accounts of Jesus. Luke said his goal was to write "an orderly account" of what happened (Luke 1:1–4). John said, "These are written that you may believe that Jesus is the Christ, the Son of God" (John 20:31). Of course, they were biased because they loved Jesus, but they did not hesitate to record the truth. After all, they even put the disciples in an unflattering light. Peter denied Christ. Thomas doubted. James and John were somewhat aggressive. Why else would Jesus nickname them the sons of thunder (Mark 3:17)? If truth were not the goal, why put anyone, especially good friends, in a bad light?

Matthew, Mark, Luke, and John are the first four books of the New Testament, called the Gospels. They are four records of the same events told from four different perspectives. Of course, all four Gospels are not word-for-word the same. If they were, it would decrease their credibility because it would look like the four men collaborated. No, these are independent accounts, and any divergent statements in them merely come from details that could easily be seen in different ways.

We have non-biblical accounts of Jesus as well from Pliny the Younger, governor of Bithynia, plus Josephus and Tacticus, who were historians of that time. So even without the Bible, we know that Jesus lived, taught, performed miracles, was crucified, and died. We know many believed Him to be the Messiah. Many believed He rose from the dead. There was an empty tomb where He had been buried. Many believed Him to be God. These are historical facts.

Consider this. There must be something to this man called Jesus, or why would we have a dating system based on His birth? BC means "before Christ," and AD stands for anno Domini, which means "the year of our Lord." Christ is the center of all history. Some non-religious types eventually began to use BCE (before Common or Current Era) for BC and CE (Common or Current Era) for AD. However, the dividing point for BCE and CE is still the life of Jesus Christ. Christ is still the center of all history.

Historian H.G. Wells said, "I am an historian, I am not a believer, but I must confess as a historian that this penniless preacher from Nazareth is irrevocably the very center of history. Jesus Christ is easily the most dominant figure in all history."[5]

Historian Kenneth Scott Latourette said, "As the centuries pass, the evidence is accumulating that, measured by His effect on history, Jesus is the most influential life

---

[5] H. G. Wells on the Historicity of Jesus | Apologetics 315, https://apologetics315.com/2013/06/h-g-wells-on-the-historicity-of-jesus/.

ever lived on this planet."[6]

Now, in my limited view, a man such as this would be worth getting to know better. And if Jesus is indeed the Son of God, His teachings become more than just wisdom from a moral advocate. They become something to believe in and live by.

C. S. Lewis had this to say about Jesus in his book *Mere Christianity:*

> I am trying here to prevent anyone saying the really foolish thing that people often say about Him: "I'm ready to accept Jesus as a great moral teacher, but I don't accept His claim to be God." That is the one thing we must not say. A man who was merely a man and said the kind of things Jesus said would not be a great moral teacher. He would either be a lunatic—on the level with the man who says he is a poached egg—or else He would be the Devil of Hell. You must make your choice. Either this man was and is the Son of God, or else a madman or something worse. You can shut Him up for a fool, you can spit at Him and kill Him as a demon, or you can fall at His feet and call Him Lord and God. But let us not come up with any patronizing nonsense about His being a great human teacher. He has not left that option open to us. He did not intend to.[7]

Choose to find out more about Jesus Christ. He is worth getting to know—from a historical and spiritual perspective!

[6] Kenneth Scott Latourette, AZQuotes.com, Wind and Fly LTD, 2019, https://www.azquotes.com/quote/544222

[7] C. S. Lewis, *Mere Christianity* (London, United Kingdom: Macmillian Company, 1960), 52.

Suggestions for practicing this choice:

- Learn more about Jesus by reading one of the Gospels (Matthew, Mark, Luke, or John) in a readable translation such as *The Message.*
- Read *The Case for Christ* by Lee Strobel.
- Read the little book *What Christians Believe* by C. S. Lewis.
- If you don't have time to read, consider getting some of these resources on CD and listen to them in your car when you commute or when you walk or work out.
- Even if you have accepted Christ as your Savior, don't assume you know all about Him. Ask God to help you know Him better.

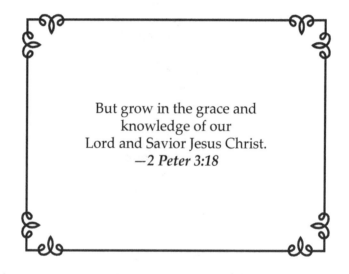

But grow in the grace and
knowledge of our
Lord and Savior Jesus Christ.
—2 Peter 3:18

Do you have any suggestions for practicing this choice?

1. _____

2. _____

3. _____

4. _____

5. _____

Choice #5
Choose to Follow Jesus

"I Have Decided to Follow Jesus" is a catchy little children's song with a life-changing message. Following Jesus is a great idea and a choice we can all make! We must simply ask Jesus to live in us, accept Him as our Lord and Savior, believe His Word, and become a disciple. A disciple of Jesus is one who follows His teachings and example.

Many do not want to follow Jesus because they think it would cramp their style. They make assumptions about what Christ would do. Sure, they believe that loving God and loving their fellow man are great principles to live by, but they don't want to be self-righteous, judgmental hypocrites like so many Christians they have known. If that's what followers of Christ look like, they would just as soon follow someone else.

However, perhaps these Christians are following a preconceived idea of what they think Christ was like. Have they really taken the time to truly get to know Him? I submit that we could all use a refresher course on getting to know Christ better. A good place to start would be to read or reread the Gospels which record what Jesus taught and did while He was here on earth.

A little research will show that Jesus wasn't a pseudo-sanctimonious recluse preaching platitudes. He enjoyed life. In fact, he came eating, drinking, and participating in life at that time (Luke 7:34). He associated with

31

everyone including tax collectors, prostitutes, scribes, and sinners, so they called him a glutton and a drunkard (Matthew 9:10–11; Luke 5:27–30). But Christ was not a glutton or drunkard, because those would be sins and He never sinned (1 Peter 2:22). He just had the ability to have a good time and relate to people of all walks of life without sinning!

If Jesus walked the earth today, would He drink a beer? Maybe. After all, His first miracle was turning water into wine. Did He do that but not have a drink Himself? I doubt it—but drinking an alcoholic beverage and getting drunk are two different things (John 2:1–10, Matthew 11:19).

Would Jesus hang around with sinners? Maybe. He did in biblical times. In fact, He was called a friend to sinners (Matthew 11:19).

Would Jesus get angry? Maybe. Anger, in itself, is not wrong, but the wrong use of anger is. The Bible says, "Be angry and sin not" (Ephesians 4:26). Jesus turned over the tables of the moneychangers outside the temple, which indicates he was a tad bit upset (Matthew 21:12, Mark 11:15).

Would Jesus get frustrated? Maybe. He seemed irritated with three of the disciples when He took them on the mountain so He could pray and they kept falling asleep (Matthew 26:40).

Would Jesus confuse the issue? Maybe. He certainly did when He said those who don't eat my flesh and drink my blood have no part of me. That was controversial for the time. Many left His side that day because they thought He was speaking literally (John 6:53–66).

Would Jesus have modern ideas? Maybe. He was certainly progressive for His time. He treated all people, even Samaritans and women, with dignity and respect. That was unheard of in those days (John 4:7–9).

Let's not put Jesus in a box and presumptuously tell others what He would or would not do in a given situation if we haven't done our homework. Our Lord and Savior emptied Himself of His divinity, came to earth, lived among us, died for us, and rose again. He did not come to condemn the world. He came so the world could have salvation (John 3:17).

Consider this. Christ came preaching the good news for everyday people. The only ones who had a problem with Him were the spiritual leaders of the time (Sadducees, Pharisees, etc.) who had preconceived ideas of what a Savior should look like and what a Savior would do. When we decide to follow Jesus, let's not make the same mistakes.

Suggestions for practicing this choice:

- Don't rely on preconceived ideas about what Jesus would do in any given situation. Find out by reading one of the Gospels
  (Matthew, Mark, Luke, or John).
- Choose to follow Jesus. That means He needs to be ahead of you, guiding the way. Keep your eyes focused on Him
  (Hebrews 12:2).
- Refrain from judging Christians who talk the talk but have difficulty walking the walk. We all have trouble in that area from time to time.
- Try not to be self-righteous. Hate the sin, but not the sinner. I know it's easier said than done, but shouldn't that be the goal?
- Get a children's CD of Bible songs for kids and listen to it now and then. Sing along! You don't even have to know how to carry a tune. We can learn a lot from children's

songs. They are short, to the point, and usually have a great message. Have you decided to follow Jesus?

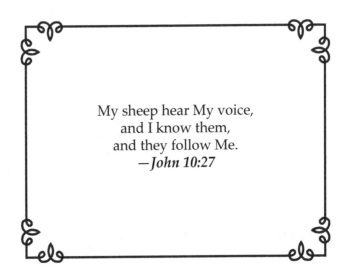

My sheep hear My voice,
and I know them,
and they follow Me.
—*John 10:27*

Do you have any suggestions for practicing this choice?

1. _____

2. _____

3. _____

4. _____

5. _____

Choice #6
Choose to Accept God's Love

We miss the mark by thinking God's love for us depends on how good we are or what we do. Many think they must change before God loves them. Nothing could be further from the truth. God loves the real us! We might want to make some changes in our lives, but we don't have to change to earn God's love.

We live in a society that constantly tells us we are not lovable. The media bombards us with subliminal messages. We are programmed to believe we aren't thin enough, pretty enough, smart enough, talented enough, or good enough. We evaluate ourselves by lofty, unattainable standards. Let's face it—even the most beautiful movie stars are airbrushed and sometimes enhanced when they appear on a magazine cover.

These false criteria can lead us to have poor opinions of ourselves. What we think about ourselves can influence how we live our lives. This is sad, because what we think about ourselves, what others think about us, and what we think others think about us can all be inaccurate gauges of reality. There will always be someone better looking, more popular, and thinner than us. Guess what? That's okay. God created you to be you and me to be me.

I find wisdom in the adage: "Be yourself—everyone else is already taken."

Our self-worth should come from what God thinks of us—and God loves us. God doesn't love us because we are pretty, smart, wise, talented, or good. We don't have to earn God's love or our salvation. Salvation is a gift from God (Ephesians 2:8). If it were based on our actions, we would try to take the credit. We would think our good deeds earned us salvation.

How wise God is! He knew we could never be good enough to deserve His love, so He just gives it to us. Martin Luther once wrote, "The most damnable and pernicious heresy that has ever plagued the mind of man is the idea that somehow he could make himself good enough to deserve to live with an all-holy God."[8]

In New Testament times, people kept thinking they needed to do something to earn God's free grace. Such was the case with circumcision. Paul wanted to set the record straight. Becoming circumcised would not earn God's love. That way of thinking devalues God's gift (Galatians 5).

Consider this. God loves us so much He sent His Son to die for us that we might be saved. We did not earn His love. It was freely given (John 3:16; Romans 5:8). We will never be good enough. You see, it's not about our goodness; it's about God's love.

People spend a lot of time perfecting an image so they will be lovable. I guess it's hard to believe that someone could love the real us, but God does. And He longs to have a relationship with us. I know it's hard to believe, but God knows our weaknesses and frailties and loves us anyway. We don't have to pretend to be something we are not.

So let's get real with God and let Him lavish His love on us.

---

[8] Martin Luther. AZQuotes.com, Wind and Fly LTD, 2019, https://www.azquotes.com/quote/823799

Suggestions for practicing this choice:

- Don't try to be something you are not—be yourself. Everyone else is taken.
- Don't use the fact that God loves you regardless as an excuse to be a jerk. God may love and accept you, but others might not if you are a schmuck!
- Remember this: God loves you unconditionally, but He also loves the other guy, too.
- Since God loves that other guy, why not try to love him, too, and cut him a little slack now and then.
- Occasionally, say, "Thank you, God, for your love!"

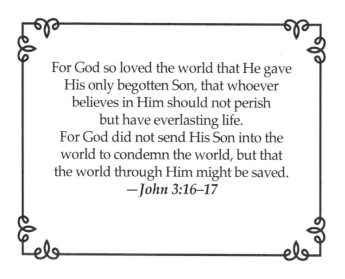

For God so loved the world that He gave
His only begotten Son, that whoever
believes in Him should not perish
but have everlasting life.
For God did not send His Son into the
world to condemn the world, but that
the world through Him might be saved.
—*John 3:16–17*

Do you have any suggestions for practicing this choice?

1. _____

2. _____

3. _____

4. _____

5. _____

Choice #7
Choose to Work Out Your Own Salvation

Hopefully, we all know that God has forgiven us for our sins—past, present, and future. Nothing we can do will ever earn us salvation because it is a gift from God (Ephesians 2:8). Nothing we can do will make God love us any more than He does. Christians who perform lists of do's and don'ts trying to get God to love them do not understand God's grace. God's love is freely given to us!

Since our salvation is not earned through our works and is guaranteed—a done deal—some would have Christians think they have no responsibility to make changes that reflect their life in Christ. I think they miss the mark. Paul clearly states we are to "work out our own salvation" (Philippians 2:12). Note that this verse does not say to work "for" our salvation, but rather it says to "work out our salvation." But what exactly does that mean?

Consider this. While it's true that good works do not produce salvation, shouldn't salvation produce good works? We are specifically told that we are saved by grace, not by works (Ephesians 2:8–9). However, in the very next verse, we are told we were created to do good works (Ephesians 2:10). So, although we are not saved by our works, we should be doing good works. Maybe that's why the Bible tells us to be doers of the word, not hearers only (James 1:22). As we read the next few Scriptures in James, we see that if we don't live as Christ would have us live, we soon forget who we are (James 1:23–24). Also, when we walk with God and try to live a Christian life, we are blessed (James 1:25).

God wants us to do what He tells us to do for our own happiness. "If you know these things, happy are you if you do them" (John 13:17). Not only will we be happy, but we will gain wisdom (Matthew 7:24).

When we look at the whole passage about working out our salvation, we see Paul telling the Philippians that he's no longer there to guide and set an example for them (Philippians 2:12–13). They are on their own. So they need to practice what they have learned from him. They need to work out their salvation without Paul standing over them and saying, "Better rethink what you are doing. That may not be a good idea." In other words, think it through. Make wise choices. And then he adds "with fear and trembling." "Work out your salvation with fear and trembling." That's just a fancy way of saying, "Hey, don't take this lightly. It's serious stuff!"

Then he continues, "For it is God that works in you both to will and to do for His good pleasure" (Philippians 2:13). Which is a way of saying, "You may do some of the work, but God gets all the credit because you cannot do it without Him."

We cannot save ourselves. God does that. We cannot do what God does, and God will not do for us what we can do for ourselves. He will not give us good habits or moral character. He will not force us to walk with Him. He will help us, but He won't do it for us. We must "work out our own salvation." In other words, God gives us salvation, and we work out what we will do with it.

Christians are expected to grow spiritually. Technically we need to grow up spiritually and stop being whiny babies (Ephesians 4:15–16). "Wah, wah, wah . . . I wanna say I'm a Christian, but I don't wanna do Christian stuff!" (Hebrews 5:12) Well, words are cheap, baby! Our actions are evidence of our identity in Christ. With God's help, we need to walk the walk, not just talk the talk.

Here's the deal. We've been given salvation, now what are we going to do with it? Perhaps we should try to live a life worthy of our calling (Ephesians 4:1).

Suggestions for practicing this choice:

- Stay close to God through prayer and ask Him to guide your Christian walk with Him.
- Read God's Word, especially the New Testament, and ask God to help you personalize what it says.
- Keep a spiritual diary where you write down what God has been teaching you.
- Don't be so hard on yourself. Think of how far you've come, not how far you have to go.
- When you fall down and make mistakes, get back up and start all over again. We are not perfect, and God doesn't expect us to be. If we could do it all ourselves, we wouldn't need God.

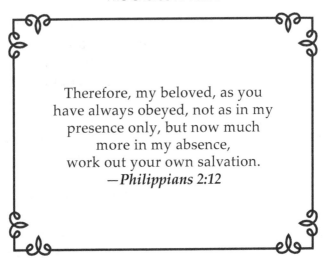

Therefore, my beloved, as you
have always obeyed, not as in my
presence only, but now much
more in my absence,
work out your own salvation.
—*Philippians 2:12*

Do you have any suggestions for practicing this choice?

1. _____

2. _____

3. _____

4. _____

5. _____

Choice #8

Choose to Practice, Practice, Practice

Christians know they are saved by grace, not by works (Ephesians 2:8–9). Salvation is a gift from God. If we could earn salvation, we wouldn't need God to give it to us. And if we could earn it, we would take all the credit. We would boast about how great we are. There are no "work-oriented" requirements we must meet to assure forgiveness. There is no checklist of dos and don'ts that will make God love us more.

Yet, we are admonished to integrate Christian principles into our lives. Why? So we can gain wisdom (Matthew 7:24). So we can be happy (John 13:17). So we can be constantly reminded of our identity in Christ. So we don't forget who we are (James 1:22–23). So we can be blessed (James 1:24). So we can be a blessing to others.

Integrating Christian principles into our lives takes effort. Paul said that mature Christians have "trained themselves to distinguish good from evil" by the constant use of what they have learned (Hebrews 5:14 NIV). Timothy was told to train himself in godliness (1 Timothy 4:7). We also need to train ourselves to consciously and consistently use what we've learned.

Use it or lose it, as they say! God will not do for us what we can do for ourselves. God will not automatically give us good habits or self-discipline. God will not force moral character upon us. We get these things by actively practicing the Christian principles we've been taught, so we can reflect Jesus Christ.

Paul said, "Whatever you have learned or received or heard from me, or seen in me—put into practice" (Philippians 4:9 NIV). Practice, practice, practice. They say practice makes perfect. I'm not sure perfection is the goal. However, the more we practice Christian principles, the easier it is to keep them integrated into our lives.

In *Streams in the Desert*, L. B. Cowman refers to a quote from the great pianist Arthur Rubinstein who once said, "If I neglect practicing one day, I notice; two days, my friends notice; three days, the public notices."[9] A parallel to the Christian life applies here.

Consider this. Why would God save us so we can remain in our old way of life? That's one of the things God is saving us from. God saves bad people (all of us are bad people in one way or another) so we can become good (better). Why? So we can lead happier, healthier, and more productive lives. That's what God desires for us, but we must do our part to achieve it.

Life is our spiritual training ground. So actively practice, practice, practice! Practice integrating what God has taught you into your daily routine. You'll be happier—and so will everyone around you.

Suggestions for practicing this choice:

- Think about one of your weaknesses (we all have them) and practice being attuned to opportunities to improve in that area—one day at a time.
- For one whole day, don't be a blabbermouth. Don't gossip or say anything that isn't uplifting about anyone. Find ways to

[9] L. B. Cowman, *Streams in the Desert* (Michigan: Zondervan, 1996), 38.

encourage others (1 Thessalonians 5:11).

- For one whole day, don't think everyone is out to get you. Give people the benefit of the doubt and don't impute motives (Philippians 4:8).
- For one whole day, don't get angry. Remember that he who angers you controls you. If you do get angry, don't let anyone know it. Let it be your little secret. If you do let others know you're angry, keep your dignity and don't make a horse's patootie out of yourself (Ephesians 4:31–32).
- When you're disappointed in yourself, don't let discouragement be an excuse to give up. Each day provides new opportunities to practice, practice, practice what you've learned. So when you fall (and remember that everyone falls from time to time), pick yourself up and start all over again!

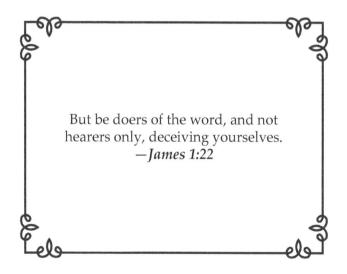

But be doers of the word, and not hearers only, deceiving yourselves.
—*James 1:22*

Do you have any suggestions for practicing this choice?

1. _____

2. _____

3. _____

4. _____

5. _____

Choice #9
Choose to Forgive

If you google the word *forgiveness*, you will find a myriad of studies showing that those who master the art of forgiveness live longer, healthier lives. This means that psychologists, doctors, and scientists are embracing an idea considered mostly theological in the past. According to the Mayo Clinic website, here are a few of the health benefits of forgiveness:

- Healthier relationships
- Greater spiritual and psychological well-being
- Less anxiety, stress, and hostility
- Lower blood pressure
- Fewer symptoms of depression
- Lower risk of alcohol and substance abuse
- Stronger immune system
- Fewer negative emotions like anger, bitterness, and resentment

So forgiveness is a good thing. God has forgiven us, and God admonishes us to forgive others (Colossians 3:13, Ephesians 4:32, Luke 17:4). However, in the words of C. S. Lewis, "Everyone says forgiveness is a lovely idea unless they have something to forgive."[10] Therefore, formulating a forgiving attitude is easier in theory than in principle. You know, easier said than done!

---

10 C. S. Lewis, *Mere Christianity* (London, United Kingdom: Macmillian Company, 1960), 104.

It might be a little easier to foster forgiveness if we know what forgiveness is not.

Forgetting

Forgiveness is not forgetting. Forgetting can possibly come with time, but it doesn't happen in an instant—like some sort of spiritual amnesia that kicks in when we say the magic words, "I forgive you." Our minds just don't work that way. Asking someone to forget child abuse or injustice is unrealistic. Dealing with it is one thing, forgetting it is quite another.

Trusting

Forgiveness is not automatically restoring total trust. Suppose a dear friend betrays a confidence but says, "I'm sorry." You can forgive the friend for the harm he caused, but to immediately trust him again with a secret would be foolish. Trust is like a bank account people build with you. It might be wise to only give them as much as they have deposited—especially if they have misused your trust before. When they wipe the fund out, they start from scratch. Trust is built gradually and given when a person proves to be trustworthy.

Condoning

Forgiveness is not condoning what was done. It doesn't approve of bad behavior. I remember when my daughter was in a group setting, and someone told an offensive joke. As jokes go, many times we don't even know it will be inappropriate until the punch line. She did not reproach the individual, but neither did she laugh. The joke teller came over to her later and apologized privately. He was waiting for her to say, "That's okay," but she didn't—because it wasn't okay. What the guy did was offensive. However, she did say, "I accept your apology." Granted, what many of us must forgive runs much deeper than an off-color joke, but the principle remains the same.

Pretending

Forgiveness is not pretending you weren't hurt or upset. That would be denial, not forgiveness. Wearing a fake smile and pretending something didn't happen doesn't make it go away. "Smile though your heart is breaking" may make dandy lyrics, but it won't keep your heart from breaking.

Preventing Accountability

Forgiveness is not preventing someone from being held accountable. One could forgive a thief who stole from him, but the thief might have to do jail time just the same. Choosing to testify against a thief in a court of law doesn't negate forgiveness. Your testimony could prevent him from stealing from someone else. Behavior has consequences. Escaping consequences is not always in the best interests of people.

Reconciliation

Forgiveness is not reconciliation. Reconciliation can grow from forgiveness, but it isn't the immediate result. You don't instantly say, "Okay, now we're all friends again. Let's be happy."

Weakness

Forgiveness is not weakness. It doesn't mean you let everyone walk all over you and take whatever life dishes out. You don't have to be a martyr for the cause. You can be a forgiving person and still say no.

Restoration

Forgiveness is not restoration with full benefits to a former position. The prodigal son was indeed welcomed home by his father. They killed the fatted calf and partied 'til the other cows came home, but his inheritance was gone. He shot his wad. It could well have been a case of "we love you, dearie, but you spent your money, honey!"

Conditional

Forgiveness is not something you do just so God will forgive you. That's like doing the right thing for the wrong reason, such as repenting just so you won't go to hell. God doesn't want us to be good just so He won't zap us. He wants us to do good from the heart. This is one of the main differences between the old and new covenant.

Earned

Forgiveness is not given only to those who apologize or earn it. Most of the people you might need to forgive may never acknowledge they've done you wrong. Perhaps they don't even care. We can't play the "if only" game. I would forgive them "if only" they would say they're sorry or admit what they did. Sure it might make forgiveness easier, but it doesn't give us license not to forgive if they don't. Christ's example teaches us this. "Father, forgive them. They don't know what they are doing" (Luke 23:34).

Easy

Forgiveness is not easy. God has forgiven us, and we need to forgive others, but no one said it would be easy. Most worthwhile endeavors are not easy. However, God is willing to aid in this process if we ask Him for help. Fostering forgiveness becomes easier when we know what forgiveness is not—and we ask for God's help.

So what is forgiveness? Forgiveness relinquishes us from feeling we are justified to retaliate, get even, seek revenge, or have an "eye for an eye" mentality.

Consider this. All of us at one time or another have had someone betray us, hurt us, emotionally wound us, or do us wrong. Humanly speaking, we think we have a justifiable "right" to hurt back or retaliate. When we forgive, we relinquish that "right." We let God take care of any vengeance He thinks should take place (Romans 12:19–21). We trust God to take care of it in His way and in His time.

On the surface, forgiveness appears to be a selfless act, but it really isn't. Forgiveness is a gift we give ourselves as well as others. Sometimes the person we are forgiving doesn't even know it. Sometimes a person knows it but doesn't care. It doesn't matter. For in relinquishing the right to retaliate, we trade caustic, self-destructive elements such as anger, resentment, and bitterness for peace. We can cross over from being a victim to being a survivor. We can get on with our lives. We can stop the past from dictating our present or future.

Forgiveness is the first step on a journey to healing. It doesn't happen overnight. It's a hard and sometimes long process but truly worth the effort. Fostering forgiveness benefits not only our physical life but our spiritual and emotional well-being as well. Forgiveness is a win-win situation. When we do it for others, we are really doing it for ourselves.

Suggestions for practicing this choice:

- When someone has hurt you, openly admit to God how it makes you feel.
- Repeat this phrase when you are tempted to feel resentful and angry: "God has forgiven me, and I need to forgive others."
- Look at the person who has offended you as a child of God—just like you.
- Ask God to help you not retaliate. Release this person into God's hands.
- Trust God to deal with this person in His time and in His way and ask God to bring you peace with this decision.

And be kind to one another,
tenderhearted, forgiving
one another, even as
God in Christ forgave you.
—*Ephesians 4:32*

Do you have any suggestions for practicing this choice?

1. _____

2. _____

3. _____

4. _____

5. _____

Choice #10
Choose to Laugh

Does God laugh? I think so. Creating the duck-billed platypus, penguin, and giraffe should merit some points on the chuckle meter. Long before animated cartoons desensitized us to talking animals, He made Balaam's donkey speak. The medical profession has come to see what the Bible told us all along: a merry heart is good medicine (Proverbs 17:22). Studies show that those who laugh live longer, healthier lives. God created laughter and it is good.

Of course, God has standards. Regrettably, people can pollute humor to something crass and crude. So when I speak of Christian humor, I am not referring to vulgarity. God doesn't stoop to such levels and neither should we. However, we as Christians could probably lighten up a bit. C. S. Lewis said that most Christians lack "merriment."[11]

Christians are a rare breed when it comes to laughter. Just the knowledge of Jesus Christ as our Savior should fill us with joy, but Christians can be some of the biggest fuddy-duddies around. Sometimes we want to determine what should or should not be funny for everyone else. That's what happened when I was attending a Christian college.

---

[11] Sharon James, "Are You Enjoying God," from *Girlfriends in God Devotionals*, September 18, 2012, https://www.oneplace.com/devotionals/girlfriends-in-god/girlfriends-in-god-sept-18-2012-11677847.html.

Each year the music department presented a program. One time they did a parody about opera. A girl sang a comic aria while she answered the phone and talked to her boyfriend. It was funny, but the administration wasn't laughing. Most of their experience with arias came from Handel's *Messiah* and Mendelssohn's *Elijah*—religious compositions. They equated this genre of music as spiritual. Their narrow view limited their ability to see the humor. Unfortunately, the music director got in big time trouble over this comic aria.

A few years ago, I had an opposite experience at a Women of Faith Conference. Here we had 5,000 women of all sizes, ages, styles, nationalities, and denominations gathered under one roof listening, singing, and praising God together. Christian humorist Chonda Pierce had us all doubled over in laughter at ourselves and our denominational quirks. How refreshing! If we don't believe God has a sense of humor, just think about all the different denominations and their ideas or foibles.

Thank God our salvation does not depend on whether we sprinkle or immerse, bring casseroles or desserts to potlucks, and use old hymnals or sing new songs. It doesn't depend on whether we fundraise with bake sales or bingo, clap our hands or keep them in our pockets, and drink alcohol or teetotal. It doesn't depend on whether we sit in pews or chairs, change too much or not at all, and use bread or crackers for Communion. And thank God it doesn't depend on whether we raise our hands to praise God or stay seated when we sing "Stand Up, Stand Up for Jesus." If it did, we'd all be doomed.

Consider this. Jesus had a merry outlook on life. He enjoyed Himself. He had wit and a keen sense of humor. How else would He come up with examples like a camel going through the eye of a needle and getting a wooden plank out of the eye? (Matthew 19:24; Matthew

7:3). Why else would He nickname James and John the "sons of thunder?" (Mark 3:17). Jesus used humor to get points across, but sometimes we don't recognize it because it's not funny today. Similarly, certain expressions we think are funny today the ancients would not. The Bible is full of metaphors, irony, hyperbole, paradoxes, and exaggerations for effect. In many ways, that's what cartoons are all about—illustrations for effect.

It's unfortunate when our limited view affects our ability to laugh, especially at ourselves as individuals or even as a denomination. Of course, we are not to be deliberately offensive with an "in your face" type attitude. However, true Christians aren't supposed to get offended over every little thing either.

Maybe it's better to accept our differences and laugh about them. Sometimes we just need to get thou over it and get on with serving God.

Suggestions for practicing this choice:

- Don't judge and condemn others just because they do things differently than you do.
- Read Proverbs 17:22 often: "A merry heart does good like medicine."
- Lighten up! Take your faith, but not yourself, too seriously.
- Smile! For one day, draw a smiley face on the back of your hand, and every time you look at it force yourself to smile. (I recommend ink, which will come off with rubbing alcohol. If you use permanent marker, you may be smiling for a month. Although, worse things could happen.)
- Laugh! If we can't laugh at ourselves, there will be plenty of others to do it for us!

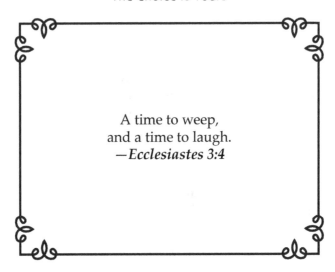

A time to weep,
and a time to laugh.
—*Ecclesiastes 3:4*

Do you have any suggestions for practicing this choice?

1. _____

2. _____

3. _____

4. _____

5. _____

Choice #11
Choose to Act Instead of React

While we may not be able to control everything that happens to us, we are still responsible for how we think, act, feel, and respond in any given situation. At times, our choices may be limited, but we can still choose to act responsibly instead of react negatively. Will we respond with strength or weakness, courage or despair, love or hate? How we respond makes a big difference in our quality of life.

When we react to what life throws our way, we allow circumstances and other people to determine our behavior. We let our emotions control what we do. Many times reacting is an auto-pilot response based on previously programmed behavior. We don't always think about our responses. We react subconsciously based on what we've always done. Old habits die hard.

However, when we act, we make a conscious choice. We have to think about and evaluate each situation. Our goal should be to do what God's Word would have us do, not what we want to do or what we feel like doing. Therefore, each circumstance becomes a learning experience that helps us grow in grace and knowledge.

Daily life is full of stress, frustration, and offense. What do we do when faced with a whiny kid, annoying spouse, or difficult boss? What do we do when we feel hassled? Do we lash out, blow up in anger, say hurtful things, or try to get even? Scriptures teach us that these are not healthy responses. They will not produce positive results.

We can determine some of our responses by planning ahead.

When we are stuck in a traffic jam, do we fuss, fume, and make ourselves miserable? Those reactions do not produce good fruit. When we drift into the habit of reacting, even minor irritants become monumental. We lose perspective. Since we all know traffic jams are inevitable, why not decide ahead of time how to act when they happen. Perhaps when a traffic jam occurs, we could plan to listen to music, listen to a book on CD, count our blessings, thank God we aren't in the accident causing the jam, pray for the person who is, or meditate on Jesus's teachings.

When someone is rude, do we react by being rude too? Do we say, "Are you always so stupid or is today a special occasion?" Or "Keep talking and maybe someday you'll say something intelligent!" If we internalize Scripture, we can determine ahead of time that we will consciously choose to be gracious even when others are not. We will be courteous and respectful to everyone—friends and enemies.

Here's a simple formula for learning how to act instead of react:

- Evaluate each situation in light of God's Word and personal core values. Using these gauges can help determine a code of conduct to live by. It helps us make wise decisions.
- Pray about it. Even quick, simple prayers can be effective.
- Think before speaking.

Choose how to act in a Christian manner. Even choosing not to respond can be a conscious, thought-out decision or action.

Consider this. Automatic thoughts which lead to

thoughtless reactions need to be brought under control. Biblically speaking, they need to be brought into captivity to the obedience of Christ (2 Corinthians 10:5). With God's help, we can control our thoughts instead of letting them control us. We do this by thinking on what is true, honest, lovely, virtuous, of good report, and praiseworthy (Philippians 4:8). Why? Because when our minds are filled with such thoughts, we are less likely to react inappropriately.

Suggestions for practicing this choice:

- Don't be quick to blame, complain, condemn, or judge others. Don't impute motives. Give the benefit of the doubt.
- Be patient with others and yourself. It takes time to change reactive habits. Ask yourself if you are overreacting. How does what you are feeling mesh with God's Word?
- When tempted to react, take a break and calm down. Don't be afraid to walk away from tense situations, take deep breaths, and count to 100 before responding (sometimes counting to ten is not enough). If someone says, "Why don't you say something?" Just say, "I'm thinking about what to say." Or "I don't have anything to say." Or "I don't think I will say anything constructive at this moment." That way, you control the situation instead of the situation controlling you.
- If you are having a disagreement with another Christian (yes, Christians disagree all the time—welcome to the real world of Christianity), suggest you both pray about the situation. If they don't want to pray

about it, you are wasting your time to get into a dialogue with them anyway. They will not want to listen to what you say.

- Stay mentally, physically, and spiritually attuned by getting enough sleep, eating healthy, exercising, and staying close to God. When we take care of ourselves, we are more likely to be able to cope with others and situations that come up.

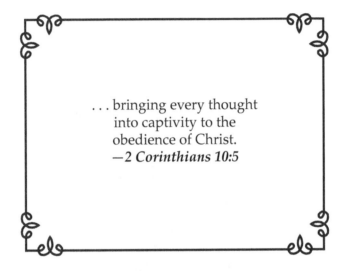

> . . . bringing every thought
> into captivity to the
> obedience of Christ.
> —*2 Corinthians 10:5*

Do you have any suggestions for practicing this choice?

1. _____

2. _____

3. _____

4. _____

5. _____

Choice #12
Choose to Keep Good Perspective

Perspective or how we see things determines how we live our lives or behave in any given circumstance.

Without proper perspective, even everyday living can become a burden. Every day we have deadlines to meet, bills to pay, and appointments to keep. We have houses and cars to maintain. We have relationships with spouses, kids, parents, siblings, and friends to nourish. Our lives are full of stress, stress, and more stress. Plus, we have those unexpected inconveniences which can be time-consuming and throw us off our game. It's overwhelming. When we get overwhelmed, it's hard to discern the difference between an inconvenience and a tragedy. This is why perspective is so important.

Do we muddle through life or look for God in all our circumstances? Do we view others as an inconvenience or as children of God? Do we see problems or possibilities? Do we focus on conflicts, or do we focus on Jesus? Do we make mountains out of molehills or molehills out of mountains? Do we discern what is most important or stay in a perpetual state of crisis management? We must focus on Christ and ask God for His peace if we are to experience the joy God would like us to have.

Keeping a good perspective is important if we are to evaluate our circumstances. A flat tire, a snoring spouse, a missed appointment, a late airplane, a lost game, the guy who cuts us off in traffic, the gossipy coworker, a criticism, a put-down, the slow internet connection, the stock market being down, our weight being up, or a computer crashing is not as big a deal as a loved one dying or finding out we have cancer.

Of course, God can take care of even the direst of situations, but we could save ourselves a lot of turmoil and grief if we didn't act like a bad hair day was the end of the world.

Consider this. A bad day is not a bad life. Before we overreact, we might want to ask ourselves if what we are experiencing will even matter to us five years from now, much less to anyone else.

In Steve Farrar's book *Family Survival in the American Jungle*, he gives this illustration. One time USC had been defeated and humiliated in a 51–0 victory by Notre Dame. Coach John McKay came into the locker room and saw a group of downtrodden football players. They were not used to losing games, but now they were beaten, worn out, and depressed. McKay said, "Men, let's keep this in perspective. There are 800 million Chinese who don't even know this game was played."[12]

Keep a good perspective. Don't look down at the ground; look up to Christ. With Christ in our lives, all is not lost! Most times, it's not as bad as we think! As Scarlet O'Hara would say, "Tomorrow is another day!" Let's get a good night's sleep and wake up with the knowledge that God loves us! Always keep this perspective in mind—with God in our lives, each day and every tomorrow can be filled with peace and joy.

---

[12] Steve Farrar, *Family Survival in the American Jungle* (New York: Multnomah Press, 1991), 40.

Suggestions for practicing this choice:

- When a problem arises, ask yourself if it will really matter in five years? Ten years? An overflowing toilet won't really impact the rest of your life.
- Don't allow disappointments to dominate your thinking for days, weeks, months, or years. Ask God to help you to "step over that disappointment" and move on.
- Look at irritants as opportunities for growth, not excuses to whine, complain, or get upset.
- We are influenced by the company we keep. So try to hang out with people who don't complain and are a joy to be around. They may not want you around if you are a grumpy goose, but more than likely they will tolerate you. Ask God to help you be a more positive person.
- Learn to laugh. We take ourselves and our situations way too seriously. Smile at others even if you don't want to. Practice by smiling when no one is around. Go ahead! Smile right now! I dare you! Smile, darn you, smile!

A merry heart does good,
like medicine.
—*Proverbs 17:22*

Do you have any suggestions for practicing this choice?

1. _____

2. _____

3. _____

4. _____

5. _____

Choice #13
Choose Substance over Style

People come in all shapes and sizes with diverse genetic, cultural, geographical, and family backgrounds. Because we are all different, our preferences and points of view may vary. Different does not necessarily mean wrong; it just means "not the same." God created us that way.

Since we are all "not the same," we have strong opinions about what we like and don't like—in all areas of life: the color and cut of our hair, the clothes we wear, the music we listen to, the foods we eat, the books we read, the cars we drive, and so on. The list is endless. You might call this our style. We all have a certain style. There is nothing wrong with that. In fact, God gives us the freedom to develop our own unique and distinctive style.

However, if we aren't careful, sometimes our style can lead to faulty thinking. The danger isn't so much in knowing what we like; the danger comes from wanting everyone to like what we like or even worse, thinking we know what God likes. Though we might not admit it, most of us secretly think God likes what we like and hates what we hate. Those who set up their style as God's standard tend to judge those who don't measure up. Sometimes, if given a choice, people chose style over substance.

We should never confuse style with substance. Let's take a church setting, for example. Some might focus more on what people are wearing, the vocal quality of the speaker, or singing their favorite song than on Christ. Believers meeting together to draw closer to God can take a backseat to personalities, appeal, and presentation—or for wont of a better word—style.

Style is a haircut or wardrobe. Substance is realizing God looks on the heart, not the outward appearance (1 Samuel 16:7). Style is how mellow or upbeat the music is. Substance is worshipping God by focusing on the lyrics sung (John 4:24). Style is tradition and ritual, which is totally different than doctrine. Substance is internalizing and living the Word of God (Matthew 4:4). Style is fine, if you don't confuse it with substance.

Some in biblical times had problems with this as well.

People didn't like John the Baptist's style. He was a recluse and lived in the wilderness. He dressed funny and had strange eating habits (Mark 1:4–6). He seemed a little severe and stark. Many didn't know what to make of him. So they called him demonic (Luke 7:33). They didn't like his style, so they rejected his substance—the message of Jesus Christ.

Christ was the opposite of John, but many didn't like His style either—especially those priding themselves on having "godly" standards. Christ was not a recluse. In fact, He came eating, drinking, and joining in the lives of those He met (Luke 7:34). He associated with everyone, including tax collectors, prostitutes, scribes, and sinners. So they called Him a glutton and a drunkard saying, "Why do you eat and drink with tax gatherers and sinners?" (Matthew 9:10–11; Luke 5:27–30). In other words, "You need to change your style." Because they could only see His style, they missed His substance— His message of mercy, grace, compassion, and forgiveness.

Sadly, today many would rather debate whether Jesus turned water into wine or grape juice (style) instead of being amazed by the miracle itself—and even more amazed by the miracle maker (substance). If examined honestly, we would probably find most church divisions come to pass because of style, not substance.

Consider this. As we grow closer to God, we realize substance is more important than style, and with God's help, we learn to differentiate between the two. After all, styles will come and go, but Jesus Christ is the same yesterday, today, and forever.

Suggestions for practicing this choice:

- It's all right to have preferences, but do not think your preferences are God's preferences.
- Do not look down on others who are different from you or don't share your point of view.
- Do not look down on sinners because, believe it or not, you are one.
- None of us want to be criticized, so practice being less critical of others. Sometimes it's best to keep our opinions to ourselves because it isn't our opinions that count; it's God's!
- Ask God to help you differentiate between style and substance.

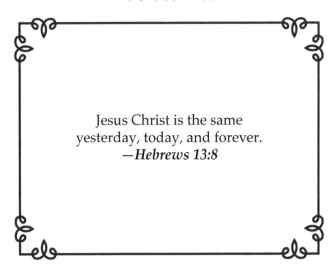

Jesus Christ is the same
yesterday, today, and forever.
—*Hebrews 13:8*

Do you have any suggestions for practicing this choice?

1. _____

2. _____

3. _____

4. _____

5. _____

Choice #14
Choose to Believe in Christ's Resurrection

Jesus tells us in John 11:25–26, "I am the resurrection and the life. He who believes in Me, though he may die, he shall live. And whoever lives and believes in Me shall never die. Do you believe this?" Do you believe this?

I think people really want to believe this. People want to believe that Jesus lived, died for us, and lives again. They want to believe that they, too, will live again after they die. They yearn for Jesus to be the resurrection and life He professed to be. Nothing brings more hope to people than Christ's resurrection because it celebrates the victory of life over death.

Yet, if you are among those who doubt this happened, you are not alone. In Jesus's time, those who chose not to believe in Christ's resurrection made such claims as Jesus wasn't really dead; the disciples stole the body to make it look like Jesus had risen; the Roman authorities removed the body; the eyewitnesses who saw Jesus were hallucinating; some saw a vision they conjured up themselves; and when the more than 500 saw Christ at the same time they were all caught up in a "mass ecstasy."

Consider this. It would have been impossible to live through a crucifixion. The disciples would not have been willing to die for a lie. The Romans would have gladly produced Jesus's body if they had it to debunk Christianity. All the eyewitnesses could not be hallucinating the same thing. And "mass ecstasy" sounds like a feeble attempt to find anything to support a losing battle.

Critics don't deny that Jesus lived. Too much evidence supports this. But it wasn't Christ's life that led to the spread of Christianity; it was His death and resurrection.

The late German Marxist philosopher Ernst Bloch said, "It wasn't the morality of the Sermon on the Mount which enabled Christianity to conquer Roman Paganism, but the belief that Jesus had been raised from the dead."[13] If Christianity was simply based on Jesus's moral teachings, it might have flourished for a while, but would have never lasted—for "if Christ is not risen, your faith is futile" (1 Corinthians 15:17). The resurrection declares that Christ is Lord. Without it, He would be just another prophet.

When Paul spoke to the philosophers in Athens, the intellectual center of the world, he preached Jesus and His resurrection (Acts 17:18). This message was so remarkable and amazing that it turned the "world upside down" (Acts 17:6). He told them God had given assurance to all men because He raised Jesus from the dead (Acts 17:31). Jesus was not some dead teacher, martyred prophet, or philosopher! He was and is the risen Christ.

Suggestions for practicing this choice:

- Do not debate with people about whether Jesus lived, died, and was resurrected. God will open a person's mind to these facts in His time. However, always be ready to answer people's questions if they ask you (1 Peter 3:15).

[13] "Rethinking the Resurrection," *Newsweek Magazine*, April 7, 1996, https://www.newsweek.com/rethinking-resurrection-176618.

- Think how God uses the resurrection to bind Christianity together, realizing that although most Christian churches differ in many of their teachings, most agree that Christ was crucified, died, and rose from the dead.
- If you have a problem with the secular aspects of Easter read *Easter, Is It Pagan?* by Ralph Woodrow.
- Repeat this often: Jesus lives, and He is with me always! (Matthew 28:20).
- Ask God to help your unbelief when doubts arise (Mark 9:24). Some disciples doubted the resurrection, but Jesus came to them to calm their doubts (Matthew 28:17–18). He can do the same for you.

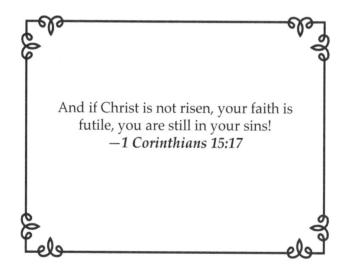

And if Christ is not risen, your faith is futile, you are still in your sins!
—*1 Corinthians 15:17*

Do you have any suggestions for practicing this choice?

1. _____

2. _____

3. _____

4. _____

5. _____

Choice #15
Choose to Make Prayer a Priority

Martin Luther said, "You cannot find a Christian who does not pray; just as you cannot find a living man without a pulse . . ."[14] Yet many call themselves Christians, but they do not pray.

The Bible is full of exhortations to pray and examples of God's followers praying. The book of Psalms shows us that David, a man after God's own heart, prayed often. He prayed when he was happy, when he was sad, when he was discouraged, when he had doubts, when he was thankful, when he woke up, when he went to bed, and all throughout the day. No wonder Paul told us to pray without ceasing (1 Thessalonians 5:17).

Jesus spent a great deal of time in prayer (Matthew 14:23, Mark 6:46, Luke 6:12, Luke 9:28, etc.). If Jesus, who was the Son of God, felt a need to pray, how much more should we feel that need? We would be wise to follow His example (1 Peter 2:21).

Prayer is not something we do when a bolt of inspiration hits us, or when we feel like it. Prayer should be a priority and something we do whether we feel like it or not. God created us to be in a relationship with Him. Prayer is the conduit to participating in that relationship. We can't really have a relationship with someone we don't spend time with.

---

[14] Martin Luther, Weimar edition of *Luther's Works*, Weimar Ausgabe WA, English version *Luther's Works* LW (Hermann Bohlau of Weimar Publisher, 1530), WA45, LW24.

Here are some excuses (not reasons) why people don't pray:

They don't think they have time. Of course, we know this isn't true. They just don't want to take the time. Studies show people spend hours and hours a day watching TV, surfing the internet, looking at Facebook, emailing, texting, Twittering, and so on. So time is not really the issue, is it? Priority is the issue.

They don't think it's necessary. Jesus thought it was necessary. If it was a priority for Jesus, it should be a priority for us.

They don't think it makes a difference. It does. *Time Magazine* has published several articles in the past ten years explaining the healing power of prayer. *Time Magazine* may not fully understand it, but they admit it exists.

People think they don't know what to say in prayer, but prayer is merely a conversation with God. Sometimes it's asking for help, but that should not be the focus of all prayer. Most times, it should be talking to God about everything that's happening in our lives and the lives of those we are close to like friends, relatives, and coworkers. It should be thanking God for every blessing. It should be acknowledging His greatness. It should be waking up in the morning and praising God for a new day. It should be going to bed at night and letting God know that you know that He's in charge—and that's okay with you because you trust Him.

Consider this. Prayer is not some magic bullet aimed at God's heart to coerce Him into giving you what you want. Those who approach prayer this way will always be disappointed. Prayer is to help align our will to God's, not the other way around. God knows what is best; we don't.

We need to make prayer a priority. We need to be praying every day. If we don't, we won't have much of a relationship with God.

Suggestions for practicing this choice:

- If you have trouble praying, read some of the Psalms out loud. They are filled with adoration and praise to God. Acknowledging God's greatness is an excellent way to get started with a healthy prayer life.
- Don't complicate the prayer process. Prayer is not contingent on saying the "right" words, at certain times of day, at specific places, and in the perfect position. These are peripheral issues and matters of personal preference. Just talk to God every day.
- Setting aside certain times to pray or having a ritual are healthy prayer practices. However, guard against making prayer more about a ritual than a heart-to-heart connection with God. That's what happened to the Pharisees. Remember that God is looking for that personal connection with you.
- We can pray anywhere about anything. However, there were times when Jesus got away from everything to have some private one-on-one time with God (Mark 35:37–39; Mark 6:45–46; Luke 5:15–16). Jesus had crowds of people following Him all the time—wanting Him to do things for them. He had to make time to pray, which is exactly what He did. We need to make time to pray!
- Pray, pray, pray every day! Pray planned prayers (Daniel 6:10, 13; Psalm 119:164). Or pray continual prayers (1 Thessalonians 5:17). Sit, stand, or kneel. Keep your eyes open or closed. Raise your hands, clasp them together, or keep them at your side. It's all

good. Start your day with a little prayer and end your day with a little prayer and pray throughout the day. Just pray, pray, pray every day! Always pray and don't give up!

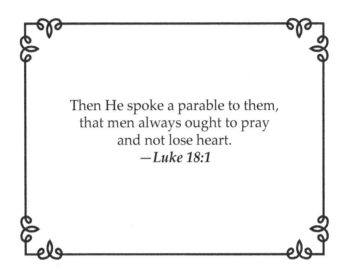

Then He spoke a parable to them,
that men always ought to pray
and not lose heart.
—*Luke 18:1*

Do you have any suggestions for practicing this choice?

1. _____

2. _____

3. _____

4. _____

5. _____

Choice #16

Choose to "Eat" Your Bible

Menelik II was an intelligent, dynamic African ruler who lived from 1844 to 1913. He established the nation of Ethiopia and is remembered for preserving the freedom of his people by defeating a major Italian military expedition. He strengthened his kingdom through expansion and modernization.

Legends tell us that Menelik II believed the Word of God had curative powers. When he felt ill, he would eat a few pages of Scripture. This seemed to work quite well for him. Then in 1913 he had a stroke and prescribed himself a strict diet of First and Second Kings. He survived the stroke but died of a bowel obstruction—probably caused by excessive amounts of paper in his intestines. If he had read the book of Kings instead of eating it, he might have learned something and lived.

I don't know if this legend is true. I do know that Ezekiel and John were given specific instructions from God to eat a scroll or two. However, we don't see any other prophets, disciples, or apostles doing the same thing. It would give a whole new meaning to the Last Supper. However, the Bible often uses the image of eating as a metaphor for studying God's Word. Jeremiah said that when God's Word came to him, he "ate" it (Jeremiah 15:16).

We are encouraged to study God's Word (2 Timothy 2:15). It is the only way we can really learn about the mind of God. Metaphorically speaking, we should devour it like a healthy meal. In our hearts, we know that spiritual food is better than physical food. After all, man wasn't meant to live by bread alone but by every Word of God (Matthew 4:4). These Scriptures were given by inspiration from God to help us understand doctrine, correct us, instruct us, train us, and equip us for every good work (2 Timothy 3:16–17). The Thessalonians were commended for searching the Scriptures daily (Acts 17:11).

We know this, but the sad fact is that most of us don't even read our Bibles daily, much less study them. However, we rarely go a day without eating because we know our bodies cannot survive without physical food. Not only do we eat daily, but the health conscious among us strive to eat a balanced diet. Menelik II found out the hard way that too much of the wrong kind of fiber could be hazardous to your health.

One's spiritual life cannot survive without the spiritual food found in the Bible. Listening to TV preachers, reading devotionals, and attending small-group meetings are great, but should not be substitutions for daily drinking in God's Word. Not only should we be "eating" the Bible daily, but in a balanced way. A spiritual diet of all prophecy will not make a healthy Christian.

Consider this. If we are what we eat, I recommend we eat our Bibles. Not the way Menelik II did, because it did not reap a healthy result. Eat your Bible the way Jeremiah did. "Your words were found and I ate them; and Your word was to me the joy and rejoicing of my heart: for I am called by Your name, O Lord God of hosts" (Jeremiah 15:16).

Suggestions for practicing this choice:

- There's an old saying in the computer world: Garbage in; garbage out. When poor or incorrect data is entered, the output is also faulty. The same can apply to our bodies and minds. So be cautious about what your body and mind feed on, so each can produce the right result. Start by feeding on the Bible before you pick up that Agatha Christie novel.
- Read your Bible daily. If you don't have time for a whole chapter, read a Scripture or two in Psalms or Proverbs. Doing this before you head out for the day can get you off to a good start.
- Participate in a Bible reading program. I prefer starting in the New Testament, not the Old Testament.
- Try reading the Bible in The Message translation. The Message translation would not be my first selection as a study Bible, but it does make the Word of God easier to understand and gives a foundational overview.
- Devotionals can give us a variety of perspectives. That's why I love them. However, be sure to look up every Scripture and see that the devotional meshes with the Word of God.

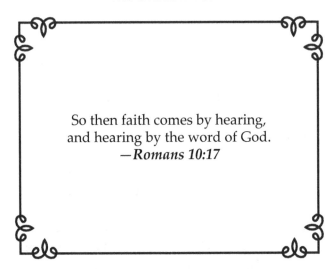

So then faith comes by hearing,
and hearing by the word of God.
—*Romans 10:17*

Do you have any suggestions for practicing this choice?

1. _____

2. _____

3. _____

4. _____

5. _____

Choice #17
Choose to Live by Grace

We can't come to Christ apart from God's grace, because we can't save ourselves. If we could, we would not need a Savior. The gospel of Christ is all about grace.

Here's the deal: We are saved by grace (Ephesians 2:5–7). This grace is a gift from God (Ephesians 2:8). Forgiveness, redemption, and salvation come from this grace (Ephesians 1:7). Jesus is full of grace and has given His grace to us (John 1:14–16). While we were sinners, Christ extended this gift to us by dying for our sins (Romans 5:6–8). Therefore, it is something we did not earn or deserve.

God loves us! Nothing we do can make Him love us more, and nothing we can do would make Him love us less. God's grace is with us on our good days and on our bad days. One would think this concept would be liberating, but for centuries, it has seemed to confuse Christians.

Most early Christians came out of Jewish background, strongly rooted in works and traditions. They were familiar with the Law of Moses, but grace posed a problem. They were used to trying to earn a place in God's kingdom by offering sacrifices, eating certain foods, and keeping certain rituals. And they were intent on having Gentile converts adhere to these Jewish traditions, too.

Paul warned the early church against abandoning grace for legalistic doctrines (Galatians 1:5). Paul encouraged living by grace rather than by works. He exhorted all believers to seek to know Christ through a personal relationship with Him. Legalism has a certain appeal because we get all the credit. We keep the law. We do it. With grace, God gets all the credit. He forgives. He pardons. He extends His hand to us. He gives us salvation. We don't earn it. He freely gives it.

Our relationship with God should be based on love, not works. Even the old covenant Ten Commandments weren't based on love. We can honor our parents without loving them. Not coveting our neighbor's stuff is not the same as loving our neighbor. Not having graven images or other gods before God is not the same as loving Him. The new covenant is about loving God and our neighbors.

The same law-versus-grace struggle exists today. People are still trying to earn their way into heaven. They strive to stay close to God by performing certain religious deeds or rituals. Such practices are not necessarily wrong, but even David understood that God didn't want sacrifices and offerings as much as a heart for Him (Psalms 51:15–17).

Humans tend to go to extremes. In the matter of grace, they either want to have a list of dos and don'ts—still trying to earn salvation—or they think since salvation is guaranteed through grace, what they do doesn't matter.

Does the fact that God has extended us grace and forgiven our sins mean He no longer cares about what we do? No, it doesn't! God forbid! Certainly not! (Romans 6:1–2). The Bible makes that abundantly clear. God did not call us to live an unholy life (1 Thessalonians 4:7). So living in grace doesn't mean we just do what we want. This grace should bring forth good fruit in our lives through the relationship we have with God (Colossians 1:5–6).

However, God does not want to guilt us into a relationship with Him. He doesn't want us to worship, pray, study, and meditate because we feel guilty. He wants us to do it because we love Him and appreciate His gift of grace.

Remember, God's grace is always with us. We stand in God's grace (Romans 5:1–2). It is with us in our daily walk with Him. Living by grace means to be totally dependent on God. God's grace is our sufficiency (2 Corinthians 3:5–6).

The law could not save us (works), so Jesus did what the law could not do (Romans 8:1–6).

Consider this. We can't afford to let legalistic practices become our life. Jesus must be our life—and our breath. Grace is not something we do. If grace were dependent on flawed humans, we would never make it. God knew that. So He decided to do it for us. Our job is to accept it with thanks and live our lives reflecting it to others.

Suggestions for practicing this choice:

- Ask God to teach you more about His grace which is at work in your life.
- Ask God to help you love Him more and more. Let loving God be the motive for everything you do.
- Because God has extended grace to you, be willing to extend grace to others.
- When you screw up, remind yourself that God loves you.
- Remember that God's grace is your sufficiency. Lean on God and trust in Him.

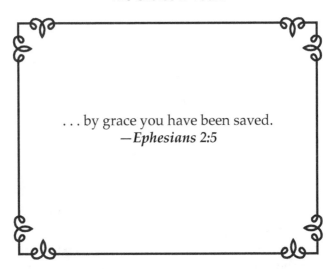

... by grace you have been saved.
—*Ephesians 2:5*

Do you have any suggestions for practicing this choice?

1. _____

2. _____

3. _____

4. _____

5. _____

Choice #18

Choose to Honor Your Parents

Did you know the biblical command to honor your parents is not just a suggestion? (Exodus 20:12). For those of us who had loving mothers and fathers, this seems like a no-brainer. Not everyone was so blessed.

My heart goes out to those who let some petty problem keep them from speaking to their parents. My heart goes out even further to those who are motherless or fatherless. The death of a parent can leave a young child feeling deserted and cause abandonment issues which can plague them for the rest of their lives.

Still others had parents but felt neglected. Perhaps a mother was addicted to drugs or alcohol. When a mother is drunk or strung out, the child becomes more like the parent. Some fathers are physically and verbally abusive. Then other parents might be there in body, but not in spirit. They just can't be bothered with raising their children. I'm not talking about single parents who are just doing the best they can to support the family and care for their children. Maybe they can't spend the time with a child they would like to, but they are trying. I'm referring to parents who detach emotionally from their children.

It is difficult to honor a mother or father who was not loving, nurturing, and kind. However, the biblical command does not seem to be limited to honoring only those parents who deserve it. A mother or father's moral character or effective parenting skills are not mentioned. So how can we honor those unworthy of our honor? Here are some ideas:

Look beyond the Surface

Try to understand why your mother or father behave as they do. This doesn't mean you have to agree with all their decisions or how they raised you, but it may help you understand them a little better.

Forgive

Forgiveness does not mean you condone harsh actions. It just means you aren't going to hold a grudge or let it keep you from being kind. Forgiveness means you show compassion even if none was shown to you. However, it doesn't mean you let people take advantage of your generous nature.

Accept

Accept your mom or dad the way they are because you can't change them. Realize that just because you understand, forgive, and love doesn't mean they will do the same for you. You do those things because they are the right thing to do.

Love Unconditionally

God loves us unconditionally, and that's how we should love our parents. They shouldn't have to earn our love even if they try to make us earn theirs. However, love should not be a guilt card people use against each other. Love shouldn't be emotional blackmail to manipulate people into doing what you want. We can love others but not agree with what they do or what they have done to us.

Pray

Bathe parents in prayer. Lift them up to God. If they need to change, God can take care of it. We can't change them, but we can choose to honor them despite their imperfections.

Consider this. No parent is perfect. If you are a mother or father, then you know this is true. Your parents made mistakes and, though you try your very best, you will make mistakes too. That's just the way it is. However, we can follow good examples that others may have set for us. We can also choose not to continue a cycle of abuse or neglect.

Honor means to regard someone with respect and let them know they have value. When we honor our parents, God enhances our lives (Ephesians 6:2).

Suggestions for practicing this choice:

- If you had loving parents, then thank God. Lavish them with praise all the time, not just once a year. Thank them for little things like passing on basic information, life skills, and common sense. The older we get, the more we realize common sense is not so common anymore.
- Don't try to change your parents. Only God can change people; we can't. Accept them the way they are and love them anyway. Remember this: Your mother is your mother is your mother. She is what she is. Your father is your father is your father. He is what he is.
- Make time in your busy schedule for your parents. Take the time to talk and listen to

them. As they get older, make sure their needs are being met.

- If your mother or father is no longer with you, then honor their memories by passing on wonderful lessons you learned from them to your children and grandchildren. Share those funny stories. Keep their memories alive.

- Say a little prayer for the child yearning for a mother or father. If you know such a child, look beyond the outward appearance and into the heart. Take the time to smile, chat, encourage, and validate.

Honor your father and mother, which is the first commandment with promise: that it may be well with you and you may live long on the earth.
—Ephesians 6:2–3

Do you have any suggestions for practicing this choice?

1. _____

2. _____

3. _____

4. _____

5. _____

Choice #19
Choose to Have the Right Motive

Most of us want to go through life doing the right thing, which is not always the easiest course of action. What is popular is not always right, and what is right is not always popular. However, when faced with a difficult choice, we need to do the right thing because it's the right thing to do.

Did you know God is interested in why we do something? Yes, it's important to do the right thing, but it's also important to do it for the right reason. The Bible tells us about King Amaziah: "He did what was right in the sight of the Lord, but not with a true heart" (2 Chronicles 25:2). Why we do something matters to God.

As Christians, we not only need to do the right thing, but we need to do it for the right reason. If we aren't careful, we can slip into doing the right thing for the wrong reason. That's what happened to the Pharisees.

They knew it was good to give offerings, pray, and do acts of kindness, but the Pharisees got off course when they did all of this to be seen by men, sit in the chief seats, and have others consider them righteous (Matthew 23:5–7). God did not like that (Matthew 5:1–5). They were doing the right things for the wrong reasons. Hopefully, our purpose runs deeper than doing acts of kindness or righteousness just so others will see and think highly of us.

Doing the right thing with an ulterior motive falls

into this category as well. We all know we need to praise and worship God. But those "gimme, gimme, gimme" prayers aren't all that pleasing to God. We must ask ourselves if we come to God for what He can do for us or because of what He has already done for us. God isn't in the business of giving us everything we want. Will we still praise Him even if He doesn't give us what we want or deliver us immediately from a bad situation?

This is a question Shadrach, Meshach, and Abednego had to ask themselves (Daniel 3). When King Nebuchadnezzar made a huge golden idol of himself and required everyone to bow down to it, Shadrach, Meshach, and Abednego refused. They would only bow to the one true God. The king was furious and said if they didn't bow down, he would throw them into a blazing furnace. He said, "Then what God can rescue you from my hand?" (Daniel 3:16).

Shadrach, Meshach, and Abednego could have gotten a little cocky and said, "No problem! We aren't going to burn up. God won't allow it!" Instead, they basically said, "We know that the God we worship can rescue us, but even if He chooses not to, we still won't bow down to your idol" (Daniel 3:17-18).

I love this story. It shows ultimate belief, trust, and confidence in God regardless of what God chooses to do. After all, God is God and we are not. Isn't that the whole lesson of the book of Job? If it is God's will not to deliver us the way we want to be delivered, is it okay with us? Or do we just pray and worship God so He will give us what we want?

What should our motive be? It can be summed up in one word—love. Shadrach, Meshach, and Abednego didn't bow down because they loved and trusted God. We pray and worship God because we love Him. We do acts of kindness because we love others. The love chapter tells us we can do wondrous works and remarkable unselfish deeds, but if we have not love, it profits nothing (1 Corinthians 13).

Love motivates us to produce works that glorify God. This is the reason to do the right thing. Everything we do should be done not so we will look good, but for the glory of God (1 Corinthians 10:31). We do it all for God's glory—not ours.

Consider this. A person should strive to do the right thing. As Christians, we need to be sure we are doing it for the right reason.

Suggestions for practicing this suggestion:

- Do an anonymous act of kindness and resist the temptation to tell others you did it. Let it be between you and God.
- Try to pray at least once a day without asking God for anything for yourself—only for others.
- Try to pray at least once a day where you only thank God and not ask Him for anything.
- Do what is right even if it is not popular.
- Ask God to help you have a pure motive in what you do.

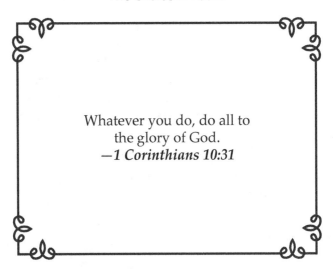

Whatever you do, do all to
the glory of God.
—*1 Corinthians 10:31*

Do you have any suggestions for practicing this choice?

1. _____

2. _____

3. _____

4. _____

5. _____

Choice #20
Choose to Be Spiritually Mature

As Peter neared the end of his ministry, he left the churches with an exhortation to be steadfast and to "grow in the grace and knowledge of our Lord and Savior Jesus Christ" (2 Peter 3:17–18). These are his last written words to the churches, so they must be important.

Growing in grace and knowledge means to become spiritually mature. God never intended us to remain babes in Christ forever. He expected us to grow up (Hebrew 5:13–15).

Babies are cute when they are little. However, twenty or thirty or forty-year-old big babies are not. Fifty-year-olds who have not learned how to share, play nicely with others or control their emotions are not fun to be around. Longtime Christians who are still selfish, undiscerning, and belligerent are not fun to be around either (Hebrew 5:13–15). Rather than mirroring how young Christians should live, some need a refresher course in the first principles of following Christ.

Maturity is reflected in our thoughts, words, actions, reactions, attitudes, and so on. Christians desiring spiritual maturity need to "walk the walk, not just talk the talk." They need to be doers of the Word, not hearers only, as stated in the book of James (James 1:22).

When James wrote this book, it was to the Christians living outside of Palestine—to those scattered abroad

(James 1:1). Nero's persecution had caused many believers to scatter throughout Asia Minor. Believers became lethargic. Their focus shifted from Jesus to succumbing to temptations (James 1:13–15). They were not practicing what they had learned. Therefore, their spiritual growth had halted.

While it is true most of us are not isolated from other Christians, we do have lots of time-wasting temptations to draw us away from Christ. Just having a cell phone, TV, and internet access can make us spiritually lethargic. Spending time with Christ no longer seems to be a priority. Has our spiritual growth slowed or possibly halted altogether?

Spiritual growth means applying God's truth in every area of our lives. It means continually seeking God and wanting to know more about Him. It means never reaching the point where we think we know it all. It means never becoming complacent. It means fixing our eyes upon Jesus and wanting to become more like Him. This is difficult to do if we aren't spending time with Him.

Consider this. If we aren't growing in grace and knowledge, we are remaining spiritually stagnant. God doesn't want us to be stagnant; He wants us to grow. When Paul prayed for the church at Philippi, he asked for their love to overflow more and more, and that they would continue to grow (Philippians 1:9). Our spiritual growth should never end.

When we aren't growing in grace and knowledge, we are not becoming spiritually mature Christians. That's what God wants us to be. Perhaps asking God to rekindle our desire to be more spiritually minded will not only bring us blessings, but it will bring blessings to those around us.

Suggestions for practicing this choice:

- Think about how much we love our children and how pleased we are when they learn a life lesson. It doesn't make us love them any more, but we are happy because they will have an easier life as they master certain self-disciplines. Likewise, we are God's children, and He loves us unconditionally. But think of how happy He is each time we become a little more spiritually mature. It doesn't make Him love us more, but He's glad because our lives will be easier and more blessed.
- Here are some keys to growing spiritually: prayer, Bible study, and meditation on God's Word. Try to incorporate those into your daily routine.
- Ask God to rekindle your desire to be more spiritually minded.
- When you encounter someone you think is a big baby (and you see them all the time), let it remind you to become more spiritually mature.
- We all have those days when we are out of sorts. When you know you are ill-tempered or overreacting, say this to yourself: GROW UP, YOU BIG BABY! You'll be surprised how quickly your attitude can change. It's even more fun to say it to someone else, but I don't think the spiritually mature Christian would do that.

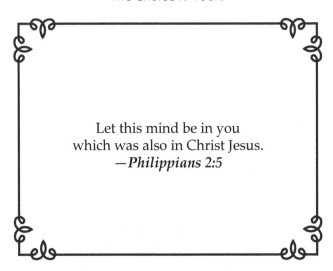

Let this mind be in you
which was also in Christ Jesus.
—*Philippians 2:5*

Do you have any suggestions for practicing this choice?

1. _____

2. _____

3. _____

4. _____

5. _____

Choice #21
Choose Not to Offend

Jesus tells us it would be better if a person were drowned in the sea than to offend a new believer (Luke 17:1–4; Matthew 18:6). Paul said, "We give no offense in anything" (2 Corinthians 6:3). The message seems clear that we should avoid offending others. Offending those new in the faith may cause them to stumble; offending non-Christians may put up a roadblock to sharing our faith.

But is it possible to go through life without offending someone? I don't think so—not unless you are living in a cave away from all humanity. Offend means to upset or annoy someone. Some people are so insecure and easily hurt we can inadvertently upset them without even knowing about it. I don't think it's reasonable or even biblical to think we can go through life without offending others. Sometimes our very presence or existence is vexing to someone. How do we get around that?

Here's a better concept of the biblical principle. We are not to deliberately offend others by being insensitive. The word for offense in 2 Corinthians 6:3 is translated as "an obstacle, difficulty, or stumbling block." We want to avoid being a stumbling block to those weak in the faith (1 Corinthians 8:9) and to unbelievers (1 Corinthians 10:32).

In biblical times, some used their newfound freedom in Christ with an "in your face" type attitude instead of being sensitive to those making the transition from old covenant teachings to the new covenant understandings. I don't think most Christians today would deliberately cause others to stumble or be a stumbling block, but they do sometimes try to change others to fit their mold of Christianity.

Paul gives some great instruction in Romans 14. If one wants to eat meat, and another wants to be a vegetarian—so what. If one wants to esteem one day better than another and one doesn't—so what. If one wants to drink wine and another wants to be a teetotaler—so what. These things have nothing to do with Jesus being Lord, Christ being crucified, the resurrection, or other basics of Christianity. They are personal preferences. These choices are neither applauded nor condemned by Paul. Jesus accepts people where they are and so should we. However, being judgmental of each other is a different matter. Paul says, "Let us not judge one another, but rather accept each other, not to put a stumbling block in someone's way" (Romans 14:12).

We need to be extra kind and gentle with others. Our goal should not be to make others conform to what we think. Our goal should be to lead a life of integrity, reverence, and incorruptibility, using sound speech, and doing good works (Titus 2:7). We need to set a good example, not a bad one.

Even so, sometimes, the gospel will offend others. Paul found that out when he preached Christ crucified. It was an offense or stumbling block to the Jews and foolishness to the Greeks (1 Corinthians 1:18–23). Yet, we can't alter the very message of Christ to appease others. We can alter how we present it, but not the message itself.

Jesus didn't alter His message when speaking to the Pharisees who were putting unnecessary religious hardships on others. He knew their hearts were not right.

Jesus was more concerned with the truth than their feelings, and they were indeed offended at what they heard from Christ (Matthew 15:12). Sometimes it's difficult to hear the truth. Correction and instruction are sometimes needed, yet it can be offensive to the one receiving it, even if it's given in a gentle manner and spoken in love (Ephesians 4:15).

Consider this. Unfortunately, no matter how hard we try, we will offend someone in our lifetime. Ultimately, only God can keep someone from stumbling (Jude v. 24–25). However, if unavoidable offenses come, let it be because truth is spoken, not because of personal preferences, attitude, approach, actions, or insensitivity.

Suggestions for practicing this choice:

- Listen more, speak less. Practice keeping your opinions to yourself. If you do speak, do so in a soft, courteous manner (Proverbs 15:1).
- Don't judge others. Work on changing yourself, not others (Matthew 7:1–5).
- Treat others with dignity and respect. Learn to disagree without being disagreeable (Luke 6:3).
- Give up thinking you must always be right. You might win the argument but lose the friend (Proverbs 18:2).
- Try to build people up, not tear them down (Ephesians 4:29).

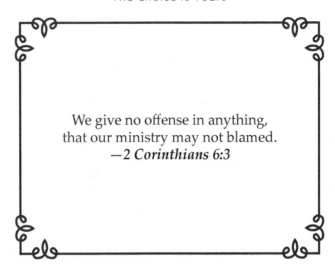

We give no offense in anything,
that our ministry may not blamed.
—*2 Corinthians 6:3*

Do you have any suggestions for practicing this choice?

1. _____

2. _____

3. _____

4. _____

5. _____

Choice #22
Choose Not to Be Offended

While it's true that we should not deliberately try to offend others, the Bible also tells us not to get offended. Being offensive and being offended both focus on self, not others. Unfortunately, our society teaches us to be self-oriented, self-absorbed, self-centered, and self-righteous. Offensive people are overly concerned about what they think. Offended people are overly concerned about how they feel. Christians should guard against both offending others and being offended.

Being offended can be every bit as wrong as offending others (Psalm 119:165). Each day is filled with opportunities to get offended. Some of us are so hypersensitive, we are an offense waiting to happen. Someone hurt our feelings. Someone made us angry, sad, disappointed, annoyed, or upset. We think someone intentionally slighted, mistreated, insulted, or snubbed us.

We take everything personally: she didn't smile at me; he ignored me; she forgot my name; no one sent me a get well card; they didn't ask my opinion; I wasn't invited; I didn't like what she said; I didn't like how she said it; they didn't appreciate my idea; they thanked everyone but me. I, my, me, me, me! Wah, wah, wah! When will we grow up and learn that the world doesn't revolve around us?

Offenses will come (Matthew 18:7). People are sometimes careless, tactless, blunt, hateful, and mean-spirited. However, most of us tend to get ticked over the little things. It's the pebble in our shoe that irritates, not the boulder in the road we know we have to go around. Sometimes people let the big things go and get bent out of shape over small, minor details.

Consider this. Being offended can be like planting a poisonous seed in our lives—one that can grow into bitterness if left unchecked. The devil uses offenses to divide and conquer. Offenses can destroy marriages, friendships, and churches. Offenses can keep us from having a positive relationship with others, including Jesus Christ. When we get offended, our spiritual maturity is revealed.

Although offenses are inevitable, being offended is a choice. We cannot change or control what others say or do, but we can control how we respond. The Bible tells us not to be overly sensitive. "Do not take to heart everything people say" because you have probably on occasion done the same thing yourself (Ecclesiastes 7:21–22). We can't let irritants and annoyances drive wedges between us and others. It hinders our relationship, not only with others but also with Jesus Christ. We are told to "bear with one another" and forgive (Colossians 3:13). Christ forgives us, and we are to forgive others.

Ultimately, we need to bring our hurts to the foot of the cross. Let Christ soothe and comfort us. Let Christ give us a proper perspective. Let Christ love the hurt away.

Suggestions for practicing this choice:

- If you feel an offense coming on, stay cool, calm, and collected. Keep your mouth shut.

A man of understanding holds his peace (Proverbs 11:12).

- Don't be a brooder and continually agonize over what offended you. This plays havoc with your mind and causes you to assume motives, jump to conclusions, and think only about yourself. Get your focus off yourself and on to Jesus. Study His Word and try to apply it to your life, not the lives of others.

- Ask yourself what this offense reveals about your heart. Are you wanting honor, approval, or recognition? Are you insecure? What are you desiring or craving that you feel you aren't getting? Are you upset with others because they did not fulfill your expectations? These are your problems, not theirs. Perhaps you should ask God to fulfill these longings or take them away if they are unreasonable. Look to God, not other people.

- Everyone makes mistakes, even you. Paul said he struggled with trying to do what was good and right (Romans 7:18–19). Believe the best of others. Don't take everything personally. Don't impute motives. Maybe the comment wasn't meant the way it sounded. Maybe they forgot your appointment. Maybe they had concerns or worries about health or family problems. Maybe they just found out the dog died. Why not give people the benefit of the doubt?

- Resist the temptation to point out every time you feel hurt over something minor a friend or loved one says or does. People say, "I know you would want me to tell you that you hurt my feelings when you . . ." Hmmm? Maybe not! They fret and fume over some little thing that was inadvertently said and then dump it on someone else. They feel better by trying to make someone else feel guilty. Wouldn't it be better just to overlook it and not make a big deal? (Proverbs 19:11). Isn't it better to think that you misunderstood or took what was said the wrong way? Isn't it better to think about all the positive things this person has done for you in the past? Don't let Satan use an offense as a wedge to come between you and others. Maybe it's better to try not to take offense when no offense was intended.

Great peace have those
who love Your law, and
nothing causes them to stumble.
—*Psalm 119:165*

Do you have any suggestions for practicing this choice?

1. _____

2. _____

3. _____

4. _____

5. _____

Choice #23
Choose to Edify and Encourage

The Bible exhorts us to edify and encourage one another (Ephesians 4:29; 1 Thessalonians 5:11). The Greek word for edify is *oikodomeo*. Technically it means to enlighten, improve, or build up. *Encourage* in Latin breaks down this way: *en* means "put into" and *cor* means "the heart." Put into the heart! These words work together for the good of others. Edifying builds someone up, and encouragement goes straight to the heart of a person.

This should not be confused with false praise or idle flattery. Not everyone is the greatest, best, or most fantastic person in the whole wide world. False praise can produce rivalry or competition, be judgmental, foster selfishness, or give a deceptive sense of evaluation. Edification and encouragement, on the other hand, stimulate cooperation or contribution for the good of all, focus on effort, make a person feel accepted, and give comfort or joy.

We live in an ultra-busy, rat race society. Sometimes we feel we don't have time to focus on anyone but ourselves. Building others up or encouraging them doesn't enter our minds. Yet, God sets us an example in these areas because He is the great encourager (Psalm 10:17; Romans 15:5; 2 Thessalonians 2:16–17). And the Bible is the most encouraging book ever written. God comforts, exhorts, edifies, and encourages us, and He wants us to do this for others (1 Thessalonians 4:18; 5:11; Hebrews 3:13).

Our motive in doing this should be love. We are told that knowledge puffs up, but love edifies (1 Corinthians 8:1). This is a fancy way of saying self-centered, know-it-all people rarely enlighten others or improve situations. However, when our motive is love for others, it is reflected in what we do and say. It is edifying and encouraging. When we build others up and let them know they are valuable, we become part of the solution, not part of the problem. We become a stepping-stone to a good result, not a stumbling block.

Here are some ways this can be accomplished:

Cooperate

When we cooperate, we don't foster feelings of competition. Learning to work together is key to getting anything accomplished. We shouldn't expect others to do what we are not willing to do ourselves.

Accept

People want to be accepted for who they are. Acceptance does not mean we condone bad behavior. It just means we don't judge and condemn. We all have areas in our lives that need changing, but being critical does not bring about healthy change.

Pursue Peace

The Bible tells us to "pursue the things which make for peace and the things by which one may edify another" (Romans 14:19). This can be done by not making a big deal out of something that is not a big deal. If we stay calm, pray, and look at something from another's point of view, our perspective may change.

Be Considerate

We can start by using words like "please" and "thank you." Give a sincere compliment. Be on time. Show up for a commitment.

Use Pleasant Words

Cursing, gossiping, and putting others down are not encouraging or edifying. We need to say only what will help, not hurt. Even when it is necessary to correct someone, it can be done constructively. Correction doesn't have to leave a person devastated. Admonition can help someone move forward.

Consider this. When we tear others down instead of building them up, it grieves the Holy Spirit (Ephesians 4:29–30). God doesn't like it. Withholding positive reinforcement from a person can leave them discouraged. When we hurt others, we rob ourselves of blessings. Encouraging and edifying others benefits us as well as those we build up (Romans 1:11–12).

We live in a pressure-filled society. This dog-eat-dog world is filled with unrealistic expectations. Satan uses this to tear us down, make us feel unimportant, unappreciated, or like we don't belong. This leads to despondency and discouragement. Sometimes we feel like Jesus doesn't even care, even though deep in our hearts, we know differently. Edifiers and encouragers are Christ's representatives here on earth. We need to let others know they are valued and appreciated. They need to know someone really does care!

Suggestions for practicing this choice:

- Look for ways to praise others. Rather than focusing on the nine things a person does to irritate you, praise that person for the one thing they do that you like. Everyone has at least one thing you can praise if you look hard enough.

- When a person is down and out, look for ways to let them know they are loved and appreciated. I've heard that one word of encouragement during a failure can be worth a hundred words of praise during a success (Proverbs 12:25).
- When a critical thought comes to mind about a person, pray for him/her. Praying for others gets the focus off ourselves and will reap more benefits than criticizing.
- Try to use a kind tone of voice and positive words when speaking to others (Proverbs 12:18).
- Pray for godly wisdom. Ask God to show you ways you can show His love to others.

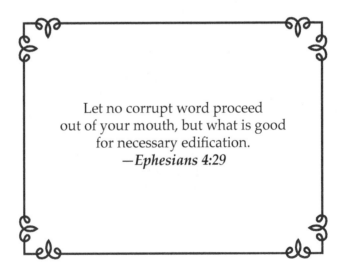

Let no corrupt word proceed
out of your mouth, but what is good
for necessary edification.
—*Ephesians 4:29*

Do you have any suggestions for practicing this choice?

1. _____

2. _____

3. _____

4. _____

5. _____

Choice #24
Choose to Hold God's Hand

The Bible continually refers to God as our heavenly Father and us as His children. I love what God tells us in Isaiah 41:13: "Fear not for I the Lord your God will hold your right hand. I will help you." If we put our hand in God's hand, He will walk with us. He will guide us on our journey.

Caring fathers exude an aura of protectiveness to their children. When toddlers are learning to walk, they want to hold their father's hand to steady their uneasy steps.

Preschoolers tend to be a little braver, so a father will demand his hand is held to keep children from wandering away, getting lost, or darting out in front of traffic. His hand gives a sense of security.

As children grow up and show a certain amount of wisdom, they might be allowed to venture out more on their own. Still, they know that a steady hand of guidance is there when needed.

Of course, there are times when teens or young adult children think they know so much more than their fathers. Eventually, as they grow in maturity, they realize dad knew quite a bit more than they thought. I heard someone say, "The older I get, the smarter my dad seems to get."

Those who had nurturing fathers find it easier to view God as loving, merciful, and kind. Unfortunately, not all fathers are that way. Some were too busy to be bothered with their children, were never around, or even abusive. Our heavenly Father can transcend those negative memories because our spiritual Father is never too busy for us. He is always available and willing to give us His undivided attention. His thoughts are only for our best. He will never abandon or forsake us (Hebrews 13:5).

Consider this. We are all children at heart. We all have times when we need someone to hold our hands. If we put our hand in our heavenly Father's hand, He will hold it. He will help us. He will steady our uneasy steps. He will keep us from getting lost. He will guide us. He will calm us, comfort us, and keep us secure.

All we have to do is say, "Father, hold my hand," and He will!

Suggestions for practicing this choice:

- Read these passages referring to God holding your hand and think about what it means: Psalm 16:11; Psalm 63:8; Psalm 73:23–28; Psalm 139:23–28.

- Think about what can be accomplished when we put what we have into God's hands. A little boy put his bread and fish into Christ's hands and a multitude was fed (John 6:1–13).

- Holding God's hand is a metaphor for surrendering our life to Him. Ask God to help you see the benefits of doing this. Here are just a few things God can do for us that we can't do for ourselves: feel loved, overcome worry, move forward, and give life purpose. Make a list of your own.

- Listen to the song "Put Your Hand in the Hand of the Man Who Stilled the Water" and be reminded that this choice is worth making. You can find many versions on YouTube.
- With our hand in God's, we can go anywhere He leads without fear. Think about this poem.

I said to the man who
Stood at the gate of the year,
"Give me a light that I may
Tread safely into the unknown."
And he replied, "Go out into the darkness
And put your hand into the hand of God.
That shall be better than light
And safer than a known way!"
So I went forth and finding the hand of God
I trod gladly into the night.
~M. Louise Haskins (1875-1957)

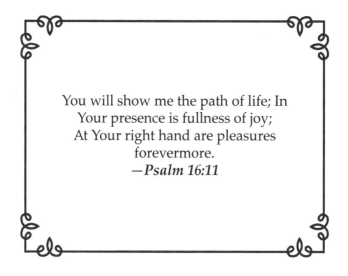

You will show me the path of life; In
Your presence is fullness of joy;
At Your right hand are pleasures
forevermore.
—*Psalm 16:11*

Do you have any suggestions for practicing this choice?

1. _____

2. _____

3. _____

4. _____

5. _____

Choice #25
Choose to Let Go and Let God

L et go and let God! Easy to say. Hard to do. Why? Because in one way or another, most of us are pack rats and hoarders. Emotionally, physically, mentally, and/or spiritually, we tend to hang on to far more than we should.

We pay a heavy price when we hang on to everything. Physically, our houses become filled with junk. Emotionally, we carry the weight of the world on our shoulders. Mentally, we become consumed with trivial matters. Spiritually, we never learn to truly trust God.

The good news is that we as Christians don't have to hold on to much of anything because Christ bears our burdens (1 Peter 5:7; Psalm 55:22). We, more than anyone else, should be able to let go and let God.

However, we don't let go because subconsciously we trust ourselves more than we trust God. Letting go means we want God to do it His way. Letting go means we trust God to do what is best. It's hard to trust because we live in a world of mistrust. So, we are hesitant to trust God. We forget that God is good and blesses those who trust Him (Jeremiah 17:7).

We can trust God because:

- He is the one true God (2 Samuel 7:22).
- He cannot lie (Hebrews 6:18). Satan lies, but God does not lie (John 8:44).

- He is faithful and will never let us down (Lamentations 3:23). That doesn't mean He always gives us what we want, but we can trust Him to do what is best for us.
- He is all-powerful but uses His power wisely (Matthew 28:18).
- He loves us unconditionally (John 15:9).
- He never changes (Hebrews 13:8).
- He can give us strength and carry our burdens (Psalm 55:22; Matthew 11:28–30).

Perhaps we have not internalized just how trustworthy God is and how much He loves us. All the things we refuse to let go of weigh us down. They keep us from living the abundant life God wants us to live (John 10:10). God loves us so much that He's willing to lift those burdens and bear them for us.

What are some things you refuse to "let go and let God" take care of? Is it anger, grief, the past, fear, a broken heart, disappointment, or disillusionment? Or is it dealing with a difficult coworker, boss, spouse, child, friend, or job situation? Could it be old habits, illness, hate, a grudge, doctrines, depression, sadness, pride, vanity, greed, or turmoil? Or perhaps it's feelings of hurt, superiority, inferiority, jealousy, envy, confusion, frustration, guilt, shame, desperation, hopelessness, or helplessness? Maybe it's being compulsive or controlling.

Consider this. Letting go and trusting God is a choice we make (Psalm 31:14). Trusting God is how we walk by faith, not sight. It protects us from worry and gives us the peace that passes understanding. Those who put their trust in God will never be forsaken (Psalm 9:10).

Let go of those heavy burdens you're carrying and give them to God. He knows what to do with them; you don't. One by one, release them into His loving hands and say, "Lord, I'm trusting You to take care of this!" Let go and let God.

Suggestions for practicing this choice:

- Memorize 1 Peter 5:7 or write it down, carry it with you, and read it every day. Learn to cast all your care upon Him, for He cares for you.
- Clean out a closet and get rid of what you have not used in the past two years. As you do this, think about some emotional baggage you need to rid yourself of as well. When one area of your physical life is tidied up a bit, it's easier to clean up the emotional and spiritual areas.
- When a thought pops into your mind about a person you have been angry with for years, pray for that person. Pray that God will deal with that person so you won't have to. Trust God to do it in His way and in His time.
- A cluttered mind leads to burdensome thinking. Practice controlling your thoughts. "Whatever is true, whatever is noble, whatever is right, whatever is pure, whatever is lovely, whatever is admirable—if anything is excellent or praiseworthy—think about such things" (Philippians 4:8).
- When you feel burdened, whisper, "Lord, I trust You." Just saying this reinforces positive thought patterns. Say it enough and you just might come to believe it!

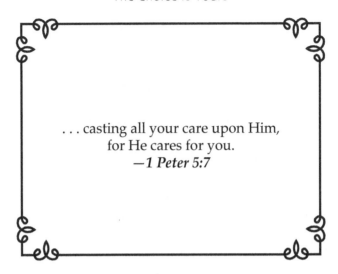

. . . casting all your care upon Him,
for He cares for you.
—*1 Peter 5:7*

Do you have any suggestions for practicing this choice?

1. _____

2. _____

3. _____

4. _____

5. _____

Choice #26
Choose to Use Freedom Wisely

Those of us who are privileged to live in the United States can sometimes take our freedoms for granted. We forget that we enjoy certain liberties that many in foreign lands only dream of. Freedom means more than just being able to do whatever we want to do. It is not a license for people to run rampant. Freedom must be used wisely.

Freedom should not be used to hurt others deliberately. We don't want to give people the freedom to abuse others, commit murder, steal, or rape. We don't want pedophiles touching our children. We don't want public school teachers feeling free to teach every new age theory that comes along. We hate getting speeding tickets, but we sort of like having those speed limits, traffic lights, and stop signs. We trust ourselves not to misuse our freedom, but we aren't so sure about the other guy!

Newfound freedom can be a heady experience. I often think of new college students. Some have not learned how to handle freedom by the time they move far away from home for the first time. Without mom and dad's watchful eye, they sometimes consume massive amounts of alcohol and focus on partying instead of education. They become prey to credit card companies who are eager to issue them new credit cards so they can charge, charge, charge their lives away! It takes a while for them to learn that they are only hurting themselves. The smart ones eventually decide to use their freedom wisely.

The Bible refers to Christians having freedom in Christ. Paul speaks of this freedom by admonishing the Galatians to "stand fast therefore in the liberty by which Christ has made us free" (Galatians 5:1). God no longer wants us to adhere to a long list of requirements to draw close to Him. Neither circumcision nor slavish obedience to ordinances, sacrifices, or rituals is any longer needed. Righteousness is no longer measured by a list of dos and don'ts. A list like that could provide a certain comfort level because following it made one feel assured of pleasing God. One never had to think about what was right or wrong—just look at the list. That was the old covenant—a physical approach to physical law.

The new covenant is a spiritual approach. With direct access to God, we don't need to jump through hoops to get His attention. He walks with us and talks with us. However, even though Paul reminds us to stand fast in this newfound freedom, we are cautioned to use this newfound freedom wisely—the way God intended. We are told not to pursue works of the flesh such as "adultery, fornication, uncleanness, lasciviousness, idolatry, witchcraft, hatred, variance, emulations, wrath, strife, seditions, heresies, murders, drunkenness, etc." Rather we are encouraged to walk in the spirit of "joy, peace, long-suffering, gentleness, goodness, faith, meekness, temperance," and so on (Galatians 6:19-23).

Consider this. Freedom in Christ does not give one license to do evil, just like freedom in America does not give one license to do harm. If anything, we should be filled with a sense of responsibility to use all our freedoms for the good of everyone.

Suggestions for practicing this choice:

- Pray for God to bless America and thank Him for the blessings He has bestowed on us that we often take for granted: the freedom to gather together, freedom of speech, freedom of religion, etc. Sometimes we don't appreciate the freedoms we have. I remember a story about a father telling his son that every person living in the United States is a privileged person. The son said, "I disagree." The father said, "That is your privilege—because you live in this country."

- Here are some things we can do to show we are thankful: be good citizens, obey the law, vote, be patriotic, etc. Try to sing the national anthem. I say "try" because the key is so high most of us have to sing falsetto, but it's our national anthem so let's sing it anyway!

- Stop looking for our country to make you happy. You are entitled to life, liberty, and the pursuit of happiness. If you want others to make you happy, guess what? You will always be miserable.

- Don't abuse your freedom in Christ by wanting the benefits without making the commitment to follow Him. To experience freedom in Christ, depend on Him.

- Celebrate! You have freedom in Christ. That's worth celebrating.

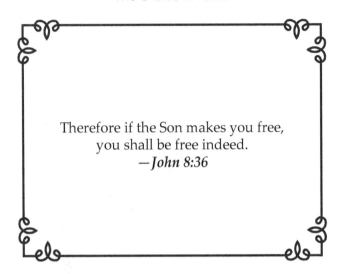

Therefore if the Son makes you free,
you shall be free indeed.
—*John 8:36*

Do you have any suggestions for practicing this choice?

1. _____

2. _____

3. _____

4. _____

5. _____

Choice #27
Choose to Love

Our society equates love with an emotional roller coaster ride or a feeling that we can't live without a certain person. Some think love is all about sex. Although sex can be a part of true love, those who equate love with sex are usually lusting, not loving. There is a difference. Love is not always about two people falling helplessly and hopelessly into an uncontrollable rage of passion. Just ask anyone who's been married for any significant length of time, and they will tell you love goes way beyond physical attraction. It's not sex that truly binds people together, or there wouldn't be so many one-night stands; it's love.

Love is something we do. In fact, love is a bunch of stuff we choose to do because love is a choice.

Love is a big thing to God. He refers to it throughout the Bible. 1 Corinthians 13 is called the love chapter and goes into detail explaining what real love is about. Here we learn some things we do or don't do if we really want to love someone: be patient, be kind, be truthful, be hopeful, don't envy, don't boast, don't be rude, don't be prideful, don't be self-seeking, don't get angry, and so on.

This kind of love can be between spouses (Ephesians 5:25), but these Scriptures can also be used as a gauge for loving our neighbors (Mark 12:31), loving our families (Ephesians 5:25), loving one another (John 13:34), and even loving our enemies (Matthew 5:43).

Unfortunately, it's not easy to love enemies, our neighbors, our families, or even our spouses because they are all people—and people are so unlovable. I'm not referring to criminals and those who perform unspeakable atrocities. I'm talking about those we may be close to and have contact with every day. They can irritate and frustrate us to distraction.

For example, some people are just angry at life and will take it out on us. Some focus on the one percent flaw instead of the ninety-nine percent good. Some insist their way is the only way to do something. Some value their opinion above anyone else's. Some can't accept that we understand their position from every angle and still don't agree. Some set up their standard of righteousness for everyone. Some gossip and say things that are untrue about us. Some think they know more than anyone else about a subject.

Some poke their noses in our business and give us unwanted advice. Some are rude and thoughtless. Some take the credit while we do the work. Some condemn others for things they are prone to do themselves. Some will make a joke at our expense. Some never apologize. Some never say, "Thank you!" Some pretend to be our friends but talk behind our backs. Some make us feel unvalued, unappreciated, and unwanted. And these are just our friends! I don't have room to describe our enemies.

Guess what! God tells us to love these people anyway—not because they deserve to be loved, but because they need to be loved. In fact, we all need to be loved, even though we are all unlovable at times.

Consider this. Loving people doesn't mean never getting irritated or frustrated with them. Loving people doesn't mean always condoning what they do or agreeing with what they say. Loving people doesn't mean we shield them from the consequences of their decisions. Loving people doesn't mean we turn a blind eye to their faults. Rather, loving people means we deal with them in a kind, patient, respectful, honest, and humble way (1 Corinthians 13). We can love people but not their inappropriate and sometimes thoughtless actions.

That's how God loves us. He knows what we've done and loves us anyway. He separates the person from the action. He can hate the action but love the person. He never says what we've done is okay when it's not. However, He never forces His will on us. He deals with us lovingly. And He knows what love is all about because He is love (1 John 4:8).

Suggestions for practicing this choice:

- Strive to separate people from their actions.
- Deal with people in a loving way.
- Try to be kind.
- Try to be patient.
- Try not to get angry.

He who does not love does not know
God, for God is love.
—1 John 4:8

Do you have any suggestions for practicing this choice?

1. _____

2. _____

3. _____

4. _____

5. _____

Choice #28

Choose Not to Despise the Small Things

W hen governor Zerubbabel was faced with the task of rebuilding Jerusalem and the temple, he faced many obstacles. Fifty years had passed since the Babylonian invasion left Jerusalem desolate and Solomon's Temple (also known as the First Temple) burned to the ground. It became obvious this second temple would never have the grandeur of the first. Even after the foundation was laid, some old-timers wept thinking of the comparison (Ezra 3:12).

Yet in this small beginning, God told the people not to be discouraged for the second temple would be completed through Zerubbabel. He also asked a rhetorical question that contains a life lesson for all of us: "For who hath despised the day of small things?" (Zechariah 4:10). The people could only see what was in front of them, not what God would do with it. How many of us are guilty of the same reasoning?

In a world that measures success by size, it's easy to think bigger is better. As Christians, we can fall into the same trap. For example, sometimes we might think megachurches do more to advance the gospel than small gatherings of people. But small does not mean weak and powerless—especially where God is involved.

God said, "Fear not, little flock" (Luke 12:32) and "For where two or three are gathered together in my name, there am I in the midst of them" (Matthew 18:20).

He didn't say, "For where two or three thousand are gathered." Of course, God can be amid a multitude as well as two or three, but having the latest technology and best acoustics does not guarantee making a greater impact for God.

In fact, God is rather adept at using small things for His glory. He sent deliverance through a little boy in the bulrushes named Moses, not a mighty army. David defeated Goliath with a slingshot, not a cannon. Thousands were fed with two fishes and five loaves of bread, not coupons for Hometown Buffet. Jesus entered the world as a helpless baby, not a powerful vision descending from heaven.

Little things mean a lot to God. Things like:

- Giving a cold drink of water to little ones (Matthew 10:42)
- Feeding the hungry (Matthew 25:43–45)
- Visiting those in prison (Matthew 25:43–45)
- Visiting the fatherless and the widows (James 1:27)
- A widow's mite (Mark 12:41–44)
- Sharing what little you have (John 6:9–13)
- Little children (Matthew 18:1–5)
- Little flocks (Luke 12:32)

The parables are full of analogies made with small things: one talent, sowing seeds, a lost coin, one lost sheep, a grain of mustard seed, and a little leaven. The list could go on.

Jesus's life was spent doing small things for others. We could call them acts of kindness. He comforted the sick. He befriended the sinner. He hung out with the fishermen. He paid attention to little children. He washed the disciples' feet. He told us if we wanted to be great, we should do the same thing—learn to serve others (Mark 10:42–45).

Consider this. God does not despise small things. He does not measure significance by size. There can be power in small things. A little match can cause a big fire. A tiny acorn can produce a giant oak tree. Little drops of water can fill an ocean. Tiny grains of sand can make a beach.

It's a big world, and in comparison, you are small and insignificant. So Satan whispers in your ear, "You are worthless, puny, and unimportant. What you do doesn't matter. Why continue? What's the use?"

God whispers, "Take heart, my child. Do not believe these lies or become weary. Believe me. Trust me. You are very valuable to me. What you do matters to me and to others. I love you and will never leave or forsake you."

In the eyes of the world, who you are and what you do may seem small and insignificant. However, in the eyes of God, little things mean a lot.

Suggestions for practicing this choice:

- Think of some little things you might do to brighten someone's day: smile, be polite, let someone go ahead of you in line, write a note of appreciation, etc.
- Small acts of faith, kindness, generosity, and service may seem to go unnoticed, but they do not. They don't go unnoticed by others, and they don't go unnoticed by God.
- Pray about the little things in your life as well as the big ones. God is interested in everything about our daily routine.
- Think about this: Adam was created as a full-grown man, and Jesus could have come to earth that way as well, but He chose to come as a little child. Little things mean a lot.

- Never think of yourself as small and insignificant. Always remember that God lives within you. With God in you, the world is full of infinite possibilities!

For who has despised the day
of small things?
—*Zechariah 4:10*

Do you have any suggestions for practicing this choice?

1. _____

2. _____

3. _____

4. _____

5. _____

Choice #29

Choose to Be Ready to Give an Answer

The Bible says always to be ready to give an answer to those who ask for the hope that is within us (1 Peter 3:15 niv). That Scripture used to scare me. Preachers have used this verse to encourage Bible study so Christians can answer questions about the Bible.

To be honest, I'm all for Bible study, but I feel ill-equipped to answer tons of Bible questions. I don't always retain what I've read. Plus, I'm not good with numbers, so I continually transpose Scripture references. I'm so thankful for internet searches and smartphones that give me easy access to this kind of information.

There's nothing wrong with being skilled in apologetics. We should know why we believe what we believe and may at some time be called upon to explain it. However, I don't think "always being ready to give an answer" means we need to know the year the Tower of Babel was built, who Meshezabel was, or how many cubits there were in Noah's ark.

Once, I was conversing with a man about some special understanding he had reached while doing biblical research. I use the word conversing loosely since it takes two people to have a conversation and this guy was not interested in anything I had to say. It was somewhat interesting, but the pontification went on for a long time. I tuned out somewhere between the genealogies, archeological findings, and where everyone had it all wrong but him.

Finally, when he took a breath, I said, "That's interesting. How do you feel all these findings have enhanced your walk with Jesus Christ?"

I expected him to expound on proving the Bible true or God's existence or something somewhat significant. Instead, he just looked perplexed and almost speechless for a moment. Then he replied, "I don't think it has."

"That's too bad," I said. "What good is all this knowledge if it doesn't draw you closer to God?" A statement he could not seem to comprehend.

Sometimes biblical knowledge can "puff us up" and make us feel good about ourselves but does not really edify anyone. To be honest, I love obscure biblical trivia, but I don't think these are the kinds of answers Peter is indicating we need.

Here's another way to look at this passage. If we read the few verses before and after, we see this section is speaking of trials, false accusations, and suffering. I like what the New Living Translation says for 1 Peter 3:14–15: "But even if you suffer for doing what is right, God will reward you for it. So don't worry or be afraid of threats. Instead, you must worship Christ as Lord of your life. And if someone asks about your hope as a believer, always be ready to explain it."

When Christians go through trials, they have something most people don't have. They have hope. Christian hope has a positive, encouraging energy that others can't quite understand. This hope is attractive to a hurting world. This hope gives a peace that passes understanding even in the worst situations (Philippians 4:7). Naturally, others would be curious about where that comes from and ask questions.

So what might people ask? Maybe they would notice we aren't reacting the way they think we should and ask, "How can you remain calm in all this turmoil?" This opens the door for us to tell them that our relationship with Jesus helps us. If they want to ask us more about that, they will. We won't need to force it or give them a crash course in salvation.

Someone might ask, "Where is your God while you are going through this?" We can quickly think about Shadrach, Meshach, and Abednego being thrown into the fiery furnace. They knew God could deliver them but said, "We know our God can deliver us from this situation, but even if he chooses not to, we will still trust him" (Daniel 3:17).

We could tell them of the promises that come through our relationship with God and that what we experience on earth is only temporary. Trials can't be compared to what lies ahead or who lives in us (Romans 8:18). Jesus lives in us!

Consider this. When this passage says to be ready to give an answer, perhaps the answer we need to be ready to give is Jesus. Jesus is the answer! He's the answer to everything!

Suggestions for practicing this choice:

- There's a difference in sharing the gospel and cramming it down another's throat. Don't force your Christian beliefs on others. Wait for them to ask questions, so you can have a natural conversation.
- Say a prayer before you answer questions. Ask God to put His words in your mouth.
- Give simple answers with a meek and humble spirit. Give just enough information to answer the question. No need to dump the whole load on them. Leave them wanting more, not gasping for breath.
- The Scripture says to always be ready to give

an answer; it doesn't say to always give it.
Sometimes people are not receptive, so learn
to read the situation before you speak up. It's
not that we need to be cautious about sharing
Jesus with others, but we do need to be wise.

- Ask yourself, "If someone were to ask me
  about Jesus, what would I say?" Think about
  that. Then you will be ready always to give
  an answer for the hope that lies within you.

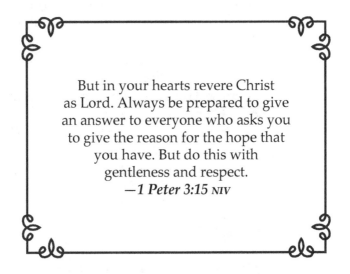

But in your hearts revere Christ
as Lord. Always be prepared to give
an answer to everyone who asks you
to give the reason for the hope that
you have. But do this with
gentleness and respect.
—*1 Peter 3:15* NIV

Do you have any suggestions for practicing this choice?

1. _____

2. _____

3. _____

4. _____

5. _____

Choice #30
Choose to Let God Be in Control

Most of us have an innate desire to control others and every situation. We say we want God in control, yet most of us prefer to manipulate others into doing what we think is best. Unfortunately, what we think is best for others, and what God thinks is best may be totally different.

There is nothing wrong with helping people when appropriate. We don't want to turn a blind eye to suffering or develop a "go and be filled" attitude when we haven't given a needed drink of water or crust of bread (James 2:16). The Bible encourages us to be concerned about the poor, the elderly, the fatherless, the widowed, and those less fortunate. But there is a difference in helping those who can't help themselves and helping those who refuse to help themselves or make changes that would enable them to lead better lives. Remember, other people have choices they must make, just like us.

We must determine when needs are legitimate. It's one thing to give a starving person a meal, but it's quite another to continually loan money to a spendthrift or gambler, get a drug user or seller out of jail, or let a deadbeat relative crash on your couch for a year or more. Yes, I know people are weak and can appear helpless, but sometimes our desire to help others causes us to intervene when perhaps we shouldn't. It's natural to want to alleviate another's dire circumstances, but in doing so, we may be circumventing the work God is doing in a person's life.

God uses difficulties to draw people closer to Him and teach principles such as "what you sow, you reap" (Galatians 6:7). When we step in and continually rescue people, we may be blocking them from receiving certain blessings from God and learning life lessons needed for physical, emotional, and spiritual maturity.

God sets an example for us. We know we are pardoned from all our sins (past, present, future)—the deliberate and accidental ones. And while it's true, God has taken away the ultimate penalty for sin—death—God does not always take away the residual consequences. In fact, He rarely takes away the consequences for our actions. God loves us unconditionally, but He usually allows a circumstance to take its course. If He didn't, we would never learn any life lessons.

Consider this. In our zeal to help others, could we sometimes circumvent the lessons God has built into a system so people will not habitually repeat the same mistakes? There is a difference between forgiving someone and continually bailing them out of situations. God always forgives; He doesn't always bail us out.

Do we really believe God can take care of a situation, or do we feel He always needs our help? We need to let God be in control. God can do it. We don't have to have all the answers. We don't always have to intervene. We don't need to react or immediately respond to every situation.

When we are the ones doing it all, we are usually proud of ourselves. Even if we give God credit, a part of us says, "Wow! Look how God used me in that situation."

Sometimes we need to get out of the way and let God do His thing. We may think we know what's best for someone, but we might be mistaken. It's one thing to provide a meal for someone. It's quite another to be-come an unappreciated, perpetual meal ticket. We want to help people, not hurt their spiritual growth. It's better to ask God to be in control and give us wisdom in each situation. He can solve problems better than we can, and only He knows what is truly best for each person.

Suggestions for practicing this choice:

- Next time you are tempted to intervene, even if that person is a family member or friend, pray about it and ask God what you should do. Ask God what would be best for that person.
- Pray for the person wanting your help. Think of prayer as your first course of action—not something you do when all else fails. One of the most important things you can do for someone is to give them to God in prayer. When you have given someone to God in heartfelt prayer, you have given them the greatest gift of all.
- Don't judge others who are weak and refuse to help themselves. This does not necessarily mean your intervention is what is best for them. Maybe you can help by listening, smiling, encouraging, and pointing them to God as you guard against getting sucked into their situation. They need your love, not your condemnation.
- Sometimes it is easier and quicker just to tell people what to do because, after all, deep down inside, we really do think we know what is best for them. However, that may circumvent their journey. Point them to biblical principles, but encourage them to list their options, find resources, and form their

conclusions. This is their journey, not yours.
- Trust God (Jeremiah 17:7–8). Ask God to help you trust Him. Circumstances come and go, but God remains constant. Trusting God is how we walk by faith, not sight. It protects us from worry, helps us wait on God's timing, and gives us the peace that passes understanding.

Blessed is the man who trusts
in the Lord,
And whose hope is the Lord.
—*Jeremiah 17:7*

Do you have any suggestions for practicing this choice?

1. _____

2. _____

3. _____

4. _____

5. _____

Choice #31

Choose How to Handle Trials before They Come

In *My Utmost for His Highest*, Oswald Chambers writes, "The typical view of the Christian life is that it means being delivered from all adversity. But it actually means being delivered in adversity, which is something quite different."[15]

God never promised the Christian life would be free of hardships, temptations, sorrow, or suffering. We are told to expect such things (1 Peter 4:12). Yet, we are always surprised when they happen.

Many think if our faith is strong enough, bad things won't happen to us. That's simply not true. Those who promote such ideas have not spent much time reading the Bible. Job suffered. Paul suffered. Stephen suffered. The twelve apostles suffered. Jesus, the most innocent man of all, suffered.

All God's children will have trials at one time or another. Dedicated Christians will face loneliness, death, anxiety, suffering, temptation, fear, exhaustion, conflict, poverty, and uncertainty—just like everyone else. That doesn't mean God doesn't love us. It's just a fact of life, and God gives a little advanced warning that it will happen.

Consider this. Perhaps God tells us to expect trials so we can determine ahead of time how to react when they come.

[15] Oswald Chambers, *My Utmost for His Highest* (Michigan: Discovery House Publishers, 1992).

James says to "count it all joy" when we fall into trials (James 1:2–4). This doesn't mean when we get cancer, we say, "I'm glad this happened." It means that trials are opportunities to draw closer to God where true joy resides. How we handle trials produces spiritual fruit in our lives (Galatians 5:22–23).

Shadrach, Meshach, and Abednego had predetermined that even if God decided not to deliver them from the fiery furnace, they would still believe and follow God (Daniel 3:16–20).

Habakkuk had predetermined he would rejoice in God no matter what happened. "Though the fig tree may not blossom, nor fruit be on the vines; Though the labor of the olive may fail, And the fields yield no food; Though the flock may be cut off from the fold, And there be no herd in the stalls—Yet I will rejoice in the Lord..." (Habakkuk 3:17–18).

Habakkuk was not going to rejoice because of trials, but he could rejoice in spite of trials because he knew God loved him, was at work in his life, and would be with him no matter what came his way. He would never have to go through a trial alone, feeling like there was no purpose to his suffering.

David said, "I will bless the Lord all times" (Psalms 34:1). This means even during trials.

We can learn a lot through trials. Trials can build our faith. After many trials, Paul concluded he could do quite a lot through God's strength, not his own (Philippians 4:11–13). If we focus on Jesus instead of our trials, we grow spiritually and develop trust, perseverance, hope, patience, and peace. These qualities rarely manifest themselves when all is going well.

We can choose how we are going to handle our trials before they come. Peter tells us to stay prepared for action and determined to focus on Jesus (1 Peter 1:13). The closer we are to God before the trials come, the easier it will be to look beyond our circumstances to Jesus. Trials can make us bitter or better. We make the choice! Daily participating in a relationship with God makes this choice easier.

Suggestions for practicing this choice:

- Make prayer a daily habit. Whether long or short, pray throughout the day. Stay in communion with God.
- Praise God continually. When you see a sunset, praise God. When you hear a child laugh, praise God. When you hear a bird sing, praise God.
- Make Bible study a daily habit. Whether it's an in-depth study, or just reading a verse or two, get your nose in the Bible every day.
- Make meditation a daily habit. Why not choose a daily Scripture and focus on how it impacts your life throughout a day?
- Thank God daily for all your blessings— big and small. Are you alive? Thank God! He wants you to live another day! And if He doesn't, that's okay too. Paul said, "To live is Christ, to die is gain." In other words, if we live—thank God because we live. If we die—thank God because we go to be with Him (Philippians 1:21).

I will bless the Lord at all times; His
praise shall continually
be in my mouth.
—*Psalm 34:1*

Do you have any suggestions for practicing this choice?

1. _____

2. _____

3. _____

4. _____

5. _____

Choice #32
Choose to Avoid Temptation

Years ago, I heard a story about an older, wealthy woman who needed a driver. She advertised and had three applicants. One question she asked each of them was, "How close to a cliff could you drive?"

The first man said he could drive within an inch of the edge of the cliff. The second said he could drive within a half an inch. The third said, "I don't know. I try not to get that close to cliffs. I try to stay as far away from danger as possible."

Who do you think she hired?

We can all learn a lesson in this story. Let's say the edge of the cliff is a temptation. Do we risk getting as close to the edge as possible hoping we won't fall off? Or do we stay away from danger?

We all have weaknesses. If we know what our weaknesses are, perhaps we should avoid putting ourselves in situations where we would be tempted to succumb to them. For example:

- If we are tempted to overeat, we should probably stay away from all-you-can-eat buffets.
- If we are alcoholics, we should probably stay away from bars.
- If we are drug addicts, we should probably stay away from drug addicts.
- If we are shopaholics, we should probably

cut up our credit cards and stay away from
Macy's.

- If we have a gambling problem, we should
  stay away from Vegas.
- If we are depressed, we should stay away
  from negative people.

Speaking of negative people, remember that who
we hang around with makes a difference. We want
people in our lives supporting our decision to stay
away from temptation, not adding to our problems.
"Bad company corrupts good character" (1 Corinthians 15:33 NLT).

Consider this. Temptations will always be around.
Even Jesus was tempted by the devil. In fact, Hebrew
4:15 says, "For we do not have a high priest who is unable to empathize with our weaknesses, but we have
one who has been tempted in every way, just as we
are—yet he did not sin." So Jesus knows what we are
going through.

Today's culture is particularly ripe with enticements,
and each day we face a myriad of opportunities to do
what we know in our hearts is wrong. However, when
given a choice to purposefully come as close to the edge
of temptation as possible, what would we do?

Remember that it is easier to avoid temptation than
overcome it. The Bible has this to say about the paths of
the wicked: "Avoid it, pass not by it, turn from it, and pass
away" (Proverbs 4:15). I think the same would apply to
temptation. Stay as far away from danger as you can!

Suggestions for practicing this choice:

- Stay close to God through prayer and Bible
  study. Pray about specific weaknesses and/
  or temptations and then look up what the

Bible says about them. For example, if you are prone to lose your temper, then not only pray about it but also do a Bible study on anger.

- If you are tempted, then flee temptation (1 Corinthians 6:18). Think about what Jenny told Forrest Gump when people were out to get him: "Run, Forrest! Run!"
- We know that God won't allow you to be tempted above what you are able to handle (1 Corinthians 10:13). However, I don't think that means we should go out looking for temptations to see if this is true. Plenty will find us without our help.
- Be careful not to invite temptation by going places where you know you will have problems resisting. When you are invited to such places learn to say, "No, thank you. I have other plans." Here's your plan: not to go where you know you'll be tempted. Remember this old joke? A man tells the doctor, "I broke my arm in two places." The doctor says, "Well, you better stay out of those places!"

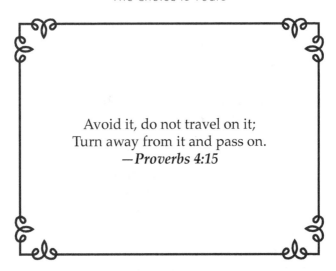

Avoid it, do not travel on it;
Turn away from it and pass on.
—*Proverbs 4:15*

Do you have any suggestions for practicing this choice?

1. _____

2. _____

3. _____

4. _____

5. _____

Choice #33

Choose to Have Unity of Faith

The idea of Christian denominations is an interesting one. Some ask, "If God is so intent on the unity of the faith, why are there so many denominations?" (Ephesians 4:13). I must admit I used to find this puzzling. How can all these denominations be right? How can all these denominations be wrong? It is an enigma.

Certain biblical beliefs are core values. These include: There is one God. Jesus is His Son. Jesus came to earth. Jesus was crucified. Jesus died for our sins. Jesus was buried. Jesus rose from the dead.

However, in other areas, much is left up to the guidance of the Holy Spirit. If the Holy Spirit is guiding people who are seeking to serve God and worship Him in spirit and truth, then we must assume there are a variety of ways to do so, since there are so many denominations (John 4:24). This shouldn't be hard to accept since God loves variety and diversity.

Unity and diversity are two different things. Christian unity involves core values and beliefs—the trunk of the tree, so to speak. On the other hand, diversity is how we choose to worship, trust, obey, believe, and have faith—the limbs and twigs of the tree.

Some call the Bible the instruction book for the saints. In that book, God has made certain instructions plain and simple, but in other areas, He has left much room for Spirit-led interpretation. To be on safe ground, we need to be praying, studying the Bible, meditating on Scripture, doing our best to implement what we learn in our lives, and not condemning others who may not see eye to eye with us on everything.

Ah, therein lies the danger! Condemnation (Romans 2:1; 14:9–11). In the past, some denominations were presumptuous enough to claim they were the "one" true church and judged others who did not agree with them in these diverse areas. However, God seems to give quite a bit of latitude in many areas even if man does not. Jesus, Himself, defied traditions and looked not to pomp and circumstance, but to a person's heart.

Some denominations prefer to worship systems more than Christ, making traditions of the past more important than the desire to change for the present or future. Others feel their way is the only way to Christ, which limits God and gives an exclusive rather than inclusive view of the church.

Consider this. When the church is mentioned in the Bible, it is not referring to a denomination. In the Greek, it is *ecclesia* which means "those who have been called out." They have been "called out" of a world that rejects God and "into" a fellowship with God and others who believe in Him. These ecclesia could very well be found in every denomination. You might recognize them because they won't be condemning others who believe in Jesus but have a slightly different way of serving Him. They will be practicing the love of God. They will be focused on the trunk of the tree, not the twigs.

Suggestions for practicing this choice:

- Don't condemn others who do not share your Christian interpretations.
- Don't compromise biblical core beliefs.

However, don't try to convince yourself that your personal preferences are core beliefs. Many areas of the Bible are hazy.

- Don't try to convince others you are right and they are wrong. That's God's job, not yours. True religion knows how to bridle its tongue (James 1:26).
- Don't deceive yourself into believing God has sent you as His messenger to persuade people to think like you do.
- Ask God to help you align your views with His.

Till we all come to the
unity of the faith.
—*Ephesians 4:13*

Do you have any suggestions for practicing this choice?

1. _____

2. _____

3. _____

4. _____

5. _____

Choice #34
Choose to Stop Obsessing about What Is Fair

Here's a news flash for you—and it's not fake news: Life is NOT fair.

While we strive to be fair, life does not always reciprocate. It's not fair when we study nonstop to maintain a B average, but the guy who plays video games all day long makes A's. It's not fair when we work harder than the guy sitting next to us, but he gets the promotion. It's not fair when we deliver a fantastic presentation, but someone else takes the credit. Life is not fair.

If life were fair, we would all have the same gifts and talents, but we don't. If life were fair, we would all be rich, beautiful, and healthy, but we aren't. While some people have worked hard for these things, others have just lucked out. Some people are born with tremendous advantages; some are born with overwhelming disadvantages. Is that fair? No, it's not, but that's the way it is.

Solomon told us long ago that life is not fair. The fastest runner does not always win the race. The strongest soldier does not always win the battle. Wise people don't always get their bounty. Smart people don't always get the wealth. Educated people don't always get the praise they deserve. That's just the way it is! (Ecclesiastes 9:11).

However, even though life is not fair, we still have choices. One choice is to wallow in self-pity. Other choices might be to put our energy into making the best of bad situations, trying to improve our circumstances, and striving to go forward (Ecclesiastes 9:10). We can be better people, not bitter. We can have peace, not anger. When those unfair things happen, do we grumble, become bitter, get depressed, and stay miserable? Those are viable options but won't make a person's situation any better. Problems are a given in life, but misery is optional.

Some people want to play the blame game when life's not fair. When they run out of people or circumstances to blame, they decide to blame God, which is a slippery slope indeed. God could have arranged things so we all have an equal playing ground, but He didn't. By human standards, we could even not call God fair. He is loving, kind, and merciful, but not what we would consider fair.

Think of this analogy: If I had a chocolate cake and eight children who wanted dessert, I would probably take great pains to make sure I cut eight pieces of cake precisely the same size so each kid would have the same portion. I know all the children would be comparing their slice of cake with the others to be sure someone didn't get a bigger piece. That's human fairness, but God is not human.

We are God's children. When God cuts the cake, He makes all the slices different sizes. Maybe we get the size we want, or maybe not. You see, God is not as interested in us getting the same portions as He is in giving us what He knows we need.

Humans judge fairness by comparing with one another. We say things like, "He's got more than me and that ain't fair!" It reminds me of the parable of the landowner (Matthew 20:1–16).

This landowner hires a group of workers for the day and pays them the going rate for twelve hours of work. Because he needed to harvest his grapes in a hurry, he kept hiring more workers throughout the day. He even hired some at the last hour. However, he paid all the workers for a full day's work. Well, naturally, those who had worked for twelve hours were upset that those who only worked for one hour got the same pay. I must admit that from a human perspective I would probably be griping right along with those who felt underpaid.

They complained. "We worked longer, harder, and in the heat of the day, yet these guys came to work for only one hour late in the day and got the same pay as us. That ain't fair!" The problem came when they started comparing what they got paid with what the others got paid. The Bible says it's not wise to compare (2 Corinthians 10:12).

Of course, this is not a true story. It's a parable, an illustration Jesus used to help the disciples understand a principle. It starts with "the kingdom of heaven is like . . ." The landowner represents God, and the workers represent us. Some of us become Christians early in our lives, and some become Christians later in life, during the last hour. Are we who've followed Christ longer upset because the eleventh-hour Christian receives the same reward? By human standards, it doesn't seem fair. But God is not human. God is God.

At the end of the story, the landowner (God) does not apologize for some oversight on his part. He says, "I did you no wrong. I paid you what you agreed to work for. It's my land. It's my money! I can do what I want with it."

Job could be the poster boy for bad things happening to good people. It wasn't fair that righteous Job lost everything—his health, his family, his fortune. Job was afflicted. Job suffered. Job was trying to make sense out of all of it. So Job questioned God. Why? Why? Why?

Haven't I done everything you wanted? Why are these things happening to me?

Guess what. God neither explains nor defends what was happening to Job. However, God does answer a more significant question Job failed to ask. Who? Who laid the foundations of the earth? Who is the Creator? Who has divine wisdom? Who is omnipotent? The list goes on and on (Job 38–41). Job never finds out why, but he does find out Who—and ends up with more faith, confidence, and trust in God.

Consider this. God is God and we are not. His thoughts are not our thoughts (Isaiah 55:8). God could control all our circumstances and make life humanly fair, but He doesn't. You can blame Him for this or accept that He has reasons for what He does. Because He doesn't always share those reasons with us, we must learn to trust Him. Our values and God's are not always the same. We may value the wages, money, prestige, or recognition. Perhaps God values the harvest, the fruits of our labor, and what we learn spiritually. Life is not fair, but keep in mind that how we deal with it can make a big difference in how we fare in life.

Suggestions for practicing this choice:

- We like it when life is unfair in our favor. Is it fair when the other speeder gets the ticket and we don't? Is it fair that we live in the United States while others live in third world countries? Is it fair that our health-nut of a friend gets cancer and we don't? Keep your life in perspective and don't compare it with others. More than likely, just as many unfair things happen for you than against you.
- If God gave us what we deserved, we'd be

dead. All have sinned, and the wages of sin is death (Romans 3:23; Romans 6:23). Always remember that God is a merciful God. Do we want a fair God or a merciful God?

- Was it fair for Paul to have all sorts of difficulties when he was doing God's work? Yet, he chose the higher ground. Instead of grumbling, he said, "We are hard pressed but not crushed. We are perplexed but not in despair. We are persecuted but not forsaken. We are struck down but not destroyed" (2 Corinthians 4:7–12). He just picked himself up and went about his heavenly Father's business.

- Remember that everything belongs to God. Who are we to question how He uses His resources? Repeat this often: God is God and I am not!

- When trials come, people always ask, "Why?" There's nothing wrong with that question, but perhaps a better question would be to focus on Who. Here's a poem I wrote as an illustration.

Why?

We go through life asking why.
Why did my loved one have to die?
Why did they choose my house to rob?
Why did I have to lose my job?
Why did the stock market take my money?
Why must it rain and not be sunny?
Why do I have to be so ill?
Why must I climb up this hill?
Why does this road seem so long?

Why is everything going wrong?
We ask these questions up to heaven.
We ask but then no answer's given.
We ask it all but we ask amiss.
The question we should ask is this:
Who made day and who made night?
Who can give the blind man sight?
Who made the mountains and the sea?
Who has a plan just for me?
Who made heaven and the earth?
Who died so I might have worth?
Who holds my life in His hand?
Who carries me in the sand?
Who knows what's best for me?
The answer's simple. It is He!
When the way seems too rough for you,
Don't focus on why, just focus on who!
~Barbara Dahlgren

Good and upright is the Lord.
—*Psalm 25:8*

Do you have any suggestions for practicing this choice?

1. _____

2. _____

3. _____

4. _____

5. _____

Choice #35
Choose to Show Loving-Kindness

We live in a rude, self-centered world. Many are too busy to show common courtesies. Courtesy is not quite as common as it used to be. The world can even be cruel—filled with bullies, revenge seekers, and just plain hateful people. How does one influence a hate-filled world?

Here's the answer: with one small act of kindness at a time. God tells us to overcome evil with good (Romans 12:20–21). God has been kind to us, and we should be kind to others (Ephesians 4:32). God's kindness should flow from us to others.

Kindness means doing good things for others. It's the act of being useful, helpful, considerate, and gracious in all situations. Kindness means we care about others—their feelings, their circumstances, their struggles, their suffering, and so on.

Studies on kindness abound. Did you know that acts of kindness stimulate the vagus nerve which warms the heart and releases dopamine into our system? Dopamine is the hormone associated with positive emotions. Kindness reduces anxiety and depression. It alleviates stressful situations.

When we treat others with kindness, it has a great impact on everyone concerned. It impacts the one receiving the act of kindness, those seeing the act of kindness, and the one doing the act of kindness. It's a win-win-win scenario. Eloquent words don't influence people as much as kindness does. One small gesture of kindness can change a person's life.

We should all strive to be kind, but showing loving-kindness goes one step farther. Loving-kindness requires us to give a little bit more to others.

I remember a story I heard years ago about a little girl who was asked to tell the difference between kindness and loving-kindness. She replied, "When I ask my mom for a piece of toast with butter on it, and she gives it to me—that's kindness. If she puts a little jam on it— that's loving-kindness."

Isn't that the way God is with us? He continually demonstrates His kindness to us through His blessings. But God doesn't just give us blessings; He gives us blessings with a little "jam" on top. He doesn't just want us to have life; He wants us to have it abundantly (John 10:10).

The word loving-kindness doesn't appear in the New Testament but seems to be embodied in the word *chrestotes* which adds the dimension of goodness, gentleness, and brotherly love to an act of kindness. It's that little something extra that lets others know we are followers of Jesus (John 13:31–35). That's why Paul told the Ephesians to be kind and tenderhearted to one another (Ephesians 4:32).

I remember Christ telling us that those who give a cup of cold water to little ones are blessed (Matthew 10:42). I often wondered why He makes a point of saying the water is cold. Room temperature water can quench a thirst just as much as cold water. I can't help but think that the water being cold is that extra love, which makes it more special. Loving-kindness goes a step further than kindness. It goes the extra mile (Matthew 5:41).

Consider this. Loving-kindness is not just being polite and mannerly. It's choosing to put a little extra love into everything we do. This type of love in action impacts those around us and helps them see Jesus in our lives.

Suggestions for practicing this choice:

- When you think of doing an act of kindness for someone, then do it ASAP. Don't put it off. The opportunity may vanish.
- It's easy to be kind when we are in a good mood, but it takes more effort when we are angry or frustrated. When those negative emotions are present, make a point to be extra nice to others . . . and to yourself.
- Show loving-kindness to your enemies as well as to your friends. That's what praying for your enemies is all about (Matthew 5:44).
- When doing acts of kindness, try to go above and beyond. Think about what you would like done for you, then do it for others.
- Show yourself some loving-kindness. Lighten up! God doesn't want a bunch of gloomy Christians representing Him.

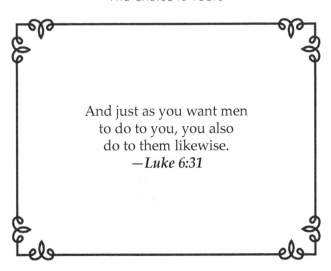

And just as you want men
to do to you, you also
do to them likewise.
—*Luke 6:31*

Do you have any suggestions for practicing this choice?

1. _____

2. _____

3. _____

4. _____

5. _____

Choice #36
Choose to Get Wisdom

Solomon was considered the wisest man who ever lived and was the principal writer of the book of Proverbs, which tells us to get wisdom and understanding (Proverbs 4:5). Why? Because wisdom and understanding are the keys to happiness (Proverbs 3:13).

Wisdom is important: "Wisdom is the principal thing; therefore, get wisdom!" (Proverbs 4:7). Wisdom is the ability to discern and judge what is good or true. Furthermore, it should lead to choosing the right course of action based on that judgment.

There are certain benefits to having wisdom (Proverbs 24:13–14). In a way, wisdom is a gift we give ourselves (Proverbs 19:8). The Bible says it is more valuable than gold (Proverbs 16:16).

So, how do we get this fantastic gift? We start by listening, hearing, and harkening to instruction (Proverbs 8:32). Let's listen, hear, and harken to what the Bible has to say about the following attributes of wise people.

They Fear God (Proverbs 9:10)

This does not mean they tremble in their boots at the thought that God could zap them into oblivion. Another meaning of the word "fear" is to have respect and awe. This is the beginning of wisdom. Wise people acknowledge God's existence and His importance in their lives.

They trust and depend on God for their needs. They realize that going against God's instruction is the same as hurting themselves; they would be "wronging their own souls" (Proverbs 8:33–36). Heeding what God says is for their own good.

They Are Humble (Proverbs 11:2)

Wise people are not know-it-alls. They are not proud and haughty. They have teachable spirits. They are willing to change and grow. They readily admit mistakes.

They Read the Bible (Proverbs 4:11–13)

Wise people "take hold of instruction." The Bible is full of spiritual instruction, and the book of Proverbs has some dandy physical instruction as well. So wise people read the Scriptures and get to know Jesus intimately.

They Implement God's Teachings into Their Lives (Matthew 7:24)

Reading the Bible is not enough. What we read must be implemented. Jesus said, "Whoever hears these sayings of mine and does them is like a wise man who builds his house upon a rock." Our Rock is Jesus Christ.

They Dig a Little Deeper (Colossians 1:9)

Wisdom is great, but spiritual wisdom is even better. Spiritual wisdom comes from a deeper understanding of God's will for our lives. Spiritually wise people can see beyond the physical into spiritual aspects of everything around them. They see God's wisdom in simple things (Psalms 19:7).

So once again, I ask, how do we get this wisdom? We mentioned that we get it by listening, hearing, and harkening, but in addition, we might try asking God for it. James says, "If any of you lack wisdom, let him ask of God who gives liberally . . . and it shall be given him" (James 1:5).

When Solomon was made king of Israel, God asked him what he wanted. Solomon asked for wisdom—not out of pride but humility—so he could rule God's people in a fair and just manner. God granted his request, and Solomon was considered the wisest man who ever lived (1 Kings 3:5–14).

Although Solomon was the wisest man who ever lived, One was wiser. His name is Jesus. Jesus spoke about the queen of the south coming to hear the wisdom of Solomon then goes on to say, "and, behold, a greater than Solomon is here" (Matthew 12:42). He was referring to Himself. What an understatement!

Consider this. Jesus is the very wisdom of God (1 Corinthians 1:24). And we who are in Christ Jesus have been given wisdom, righteousness, sanctification, and redemption. Stay close to Jesus. In Him, are all the treasures of wisdom and knowledge (Colossians 2:3).

Suggestions for practicing this choice:

- Pray for wisdom (James 1:5).
- Study God's Word and ask God to reveal the hidden treasures (Colossians 2:3).
- Seek and heed godly counsel (Proverbs 11:14; Proverbs 5:11–13).
- Associate with wise people (Proverbs 13:20).
- Read the book of Proverbs and pay special attention to every time it uses the word wise or wisdom.

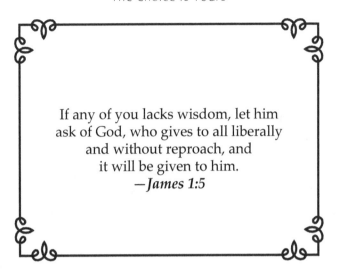

If any of you lacks wisdom, let him
ask of God, who gives to all liberally
and without reproach, and
it will be given to him.
—*James 1:5*

Do you have any suggestions for practicing this choice?

1. _____

2. _____

3. _____

4. _____

5. _____

Choice #37
Choose to Walk the Walk

Are you religious? People make a huge error thinking that Christianity is a religion. It's not so much a religion as it is a lifestyle. Religion is what you believe, but Christianity is what you live. It's something you do.

When people become followers of Christ, their lives are no longer their own (1 Corinthians 3:23). They automatically become witnesses (Acts 1:8). Others look carefully at the Christian lifestyle, so Christians are witnessing for Christ whether they want to or not. We Christians have quite a responsibility. What kind of witnesses are we?

Christians are the salt of the earth (Matthew 5:13). Are we full of zest for the life we are called to live?

Christians are the light of the world (Matthew 5:14). Do we light a candle in this world, or do we curse the darkness?

Christians are friends of Christ (John 15:13–15). Do we understand the meaning of friendship in our relationships? Can we keep a confidence?

Christians are not under the law but under grace (Romans 6:14–15). Do we know when to make an issue out of something and when to let it pass?

Christians are partakers of the sufferings of Christ (2 Corinthians 1:2–8). How do we handle trials when they come our way? Christians aren't promised a life without thorns or thistles.

Christians are a letter (2 Corinthians 2:2–3). When people read what is written on our heart, do they know more about a loving God?

Christians are a sweet aroma (2 Corinthians 2:15–16). Do we smell of fragrant perfume or reek of body odor? Do we need a spiritual bath?

Christians walk in love (Ephesians 5:2). What motivates our actions? Is it love or being in the limelight?

The main reason people do not become Christians is that they know one. By the same token, the main reason others become Christians is that they know one. Maybe we should ask, "How do people feel when they are around me? What do people see when they look at me?" I'm not talking about perfection but reflection.

When we look in a mirror, do we see wrinkles? Baggy eyes? Double chins? Scars? God doesn't see that. He wants us to see what He sees—a reflection of Himself (2 Corinthians 2:15–16). Do we reflect the fruit of the Holy Spirit or the works of the flesh? (Galatians 5:19–25). Do people see a glimmer of the reflection of God when they look at us?

Consider this. Do we profess to be religious? That may not be enough. For example, John said that just saying we love God but not showing it to our neighbor puts us on dangerous ground (1 John 4:20). On the other hand, doing something for others is the same as doing it for God (Matthew 25:24–46).

You've heard it said a million times, "You have to walk the walk, not just talk the talk." Remember, religion is something you believe, but Christianity is something you do!

Suggestions for practicing this choice:

- Remember that actions speak louder than words, so talk less and do more.

- Ask for God's help to reflect His love, joy, peace, longsuffering, gentleness, goodness, faith, meekness, and temperance in your life (Galatians 5:22–23).
- Stop cursing the darkness (complaining) and light a candle. Pray about it and see if there is anything you can do to help.
- Perfection is overrated and unachievable. Strive for progress, not perfection. Do the best you can with what you have.
- If you fall down, get back up and walk that walk!

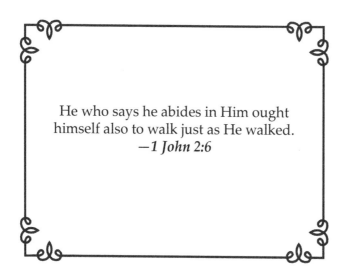

He who says he abides in Him ought himself also to walk just as He walked.
—*1 John 2:6*

Do you have any suggestions for practicing this choice?

1. _____

2. _____

3. _____

4. _____

5. _____

Choice #38
Choose to Comfort, Not Condemn

When someone is going through a hardship, they need comfort and encouragement—not judgment and condemnation. If we aren't careful, we can make false assumptions about someone else's trials. Here are a few:

A trial is God's way of punishing people for their sins. Not true! God doesn't need to punish us for sin. Sin brings its own punishment. We don't know why someone is ill. When God healed the blind man in John 9, the disciples asked who had sinned to cause this blindness, him or his parents. Jesus said, "Neither" (John 9:1–3).

People always bring afflictions upon themselves. Not true! We don't know why someone is having a trial. After Jesus told the disciples that no one had sinned to cause the man's blindness in John 9, He went on to say why this man was blind: "that the works of God should be revealed in him." We don't know what God is doing in another person's life.

If people have enough faith, they won't have trials. Not true! Did David lack faith? Did Paul lack faith? Did Job lack faith? Did Jesus lack faith? I don't think so!

Bad things happen to good people all the time, and we don't know why. And shame on those who go to suffering people and add to their misery by telling them if they had enough faith they wouldn't be going through some horrendous trial. If we learn anything from the

Bible, it's that all God's children got problems—or will have problems.

Some faithful Christians will get diseases and die no matter how many sincere prayers are said for healing. Some will be gunned down by random acts of violence no matter how pure their lives have been. Some husbands will leave beautiful wives no matter how faithful and loving those wives have been. Dedicated Christians will face loneliness, death, anxiety, suffering, temptation, fear, exhaustion, conflict, poverty, and uncertainty, just like everyone else.

People don't need judgment or condemnation when they are going through trials. They also don't need platitudes that might be helpful in the future, but certainly not during present suffering. Hurting people do not want to hear:

- This was part of God's plan.
- The Lord works in mysterious ways.
- All things work together for God for those who love the Lord.
- God doesn't give you more than you can handle.
- What doesn't kill you makes you stronger.
- You need to pray more.
- You'll be just fine.
- Cheer up! It could be worse.
- I understand how you feel.

We don't understand how people feel. Everyone is different. Everyone processes what happens differently. To say we know how someone feels is presumptuous.

Gracious words are sweet like a honeycomb and healing to the bones (Proverbs 16:24). These words are not healing any bones. If we must say something, consider statements like:

- I'm so sorry you are going through this.

- You are in my thoughts and prayers.
- Can I bring a meal over? What would you like?
- I'm here if you want to talk.

It might be better to just give a hug and sit in silence. Sitting in silence can be comforting. Here's a good guide to use: when grief is new, words should be few.

Consider this. People don't want to feel condemned or preached to in times of trouble. They just want to feel like someone cares. We can walk beside hurting people with an open mind and a willing heart. In addition, we can ask God privately to guide us so we can be a help, not a hindrance.

Suggestions for practicing this choice:

- Let people know you care by letting them know you are available if they need you. Ask them specifically if you can help by offering to drive the children to school, give them a ride, walk the dog, bring a meal, etc. If you just ask what you can do to help, they might say, "Loan me $1,000 or buy me a second-hand car." This might not be the kind of help they really need or that you want to offer.
- If people want to talk to you when they are suffering, then listen with your heart and don't take everything a hurting person says personally. Resist the temptation to give advice or say thoughtless things that will make them feel worse.
- Keep the focus on them, not you. This is not a time to compare trials by saying, "You think you got problems! I've had it so much rougher than you."

- Bathe the hurting person in prayer. God can do what we can't!
- Remember this: God comforts us not so much to make us comfortable, but so that we can learn to comfort others. Isaiah 40:1 says, "Comfort my people."

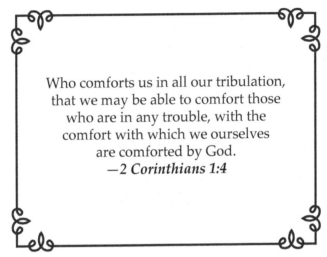

Who comforts us in all our tribulation, that we may be able to comfort those who are in any trouble, with the comfort with which we ourselves are comforted by God.
—*2 Corinthians 1:4*

Do you have any suggestions for practicing this choice?

1. _____

2. _____

3. _____

4. _____

5. _____

Choice #39

Choose Not to Get Hung Up on Rituals

After years of bondage in Egypt, the Israelites had absorbed much of the Egyptian culture. When God delivered them, He wanted them to be a separate people—an example to surrounding nations. To accomplish this, God provided them with a set of laws. If the Israelites obeyed this covenant, God said that they would be His "treasured possession . . . and a holy nation" (Exodus 19:5–6).

Therefore, the book of Leviticus is crammed full of detailed procedures, rules, and rituals the Israelites were expected to follow. Each instruction had a specific purpose designed for the time in which they lived—old covenant times. However, times change.

When Jesus came to establish a new covenant, things would be different. No longer were godly people identified by their rules and rituals. Their identity would be in Christ.

This was a hard concept for the Pharisees to grasp. The Pharisees were the religious experts of the time and the keepers of the Mosaic law. By the time they encountered Christ, certain rules had been added to the law. Many had become extreme customs—so much so that the original intent of the written law was often lost. Yet, the Jewish leaders felt the observance of these regulations were vital in keeping God's favor and considered themselves the righteous standard for obedience to God.

Jesus claimed to be the Son of God, but He continually violated the Pharisee's godly customs. For example, He ate and drank with sinners, which made Him ceremonially unclean (Luke 7:34–39). He broke the Sabbath by healing people and picking a little corn to eat (Luke 13:14; Matthew 12:1–2). He and the disciples did not participate in the ceremonial washing of their hands before they ate (Mark 7:1–23).

Now, this washing of the hands ceremony was a bigger deal than just using hand sanitizer for healthy eating. Fingertips had to point up. Water poured down them until it ran down the wrist. A palm would be cleaned with the fist of the other hand. Fingertips would then point down. Water poured down them until it ran off the fingertips. Then they would switch hands and repeat.

Shockingly, Jesus did not wash His hands that way. When the Pharisees asked him why, He replied with a quote from Isaiah 29:13: "These people honor me with their lips, but their heart is far from me. They worship me in vain, but their teachings are but rules taught by men." He went on to say, "You nullify the word of God with your tradition" (Mark 7:13). In other words, "You think your traditions are more important than the word of God!"

Christ was saying that what we do is not as important as why we do it. Jesus did not come with a list of rules and regulations. He came with His law of love.

In New Testament times, people were used to seeing works—customs and rituals—performed. So they asked Jesus, "What must we do to do the works God requires?" Jesus replied, "The work of God is this: to believe in the one He has sent" (John 6:28– 29 NIV). This was a new, radical concept.

Most of us think, "Those silly Pharisees. They just didn't get it!" How could they set up their own customs, rituals, and standards of righteousness and think they were God's?

But how many of us really "get it"? How many of us have subconsciously done the same thing, worshipping traditions more than Christ?

Are we tied to total immersion baptism or how often we take Communion? Is the order of our church service or the tempo of our worship music of paramount importance? Do we argue over what instruments are allowed in church, the correct hymnal—or no hymnal—dietary habits, circumcision, tithing, or Old Testament holy days? Are matters of hair length, Bible translations, use of alcohol, and appropriate worship attire for men and women worth quibbling over? Does Saturday versus Sunday worship, the altar call, or how an offering is collected offend us? It's fine to have opinions about these things or even continue the traditions to which we have grown accustomed. But when we focus more on what we do instead of why we do it, we miss the mark.

Even more dangerous is when we judge and condemn others who do not observe the faith the way we think it should be done. Are we using God's standard or our own? Are we doing things for God's glory or our own? Are we doing things because we think God likes it or because we like it? We need to be honest with ourselves.

The same goes for those who break tradition. Are they doing it as an act of rebellion? Are they judging and condemning those who like tradition and ritual? It works both ways.

Consider this. If a custom or ritual enhances your relationship with God, then so be it. But we must control our rituals; they should not control us. If they control us, we have no flexibility or room for anything that might be a little different—like the Pharisees.

We need to keep perspective. After all, God has

called us into a relationship, not a ritual (1 Corinthians 1:9).

Suggestions for practicing this choice:

- Do not judge others who do things differently than you do.
- Do not confine God to your standard.
- Do not use God to justify your likes and dislikes.
- Do not think of the Bible as a list of dos and don'ts.
- Think of the Bible as a way to get to know the mind of Christ. The important questions to ask when studying Scriptures are not: what, when, why, or how. The Bible is all about Who! Get to know the Who (Jesus Christ), and all the other questions will be answered or pale in significance.

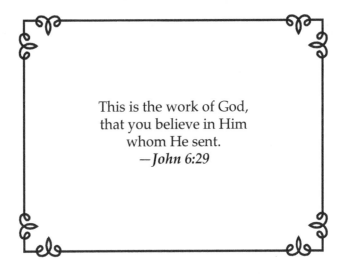

This is the work of God,
that you believe in Him
whom He sent.
—*John 6:29*

Do you have any suggestions for practicing this choice?

1. _____

2. _____

3. _____

4. _____

5. _____

Choice #40
Choose to Agree to Disagree

Psalms 133:1 says, "How good and how pleasant for brethren to dwell together in unity."

Some feel that unity is hard to achieve. I have a solution. If everyone would just agree with me and do things my way, we could be unified. I explained this to my friend. He didn't agree. He felt unity could only be achieved if everyone agreed with him and did it his way. What a dilemma!

God created us to be different. We have different eyes and hair, shapes and sizes, backgrounds and environments, likes and dislikes. It would be reasonable to assume that we have different points of view and opinions.

We are individuals, and God deals with us as individuals. Individuality can be a great thing. However, when we try to work with others, being an individualist can divide us, not unite us. God's Spirit is more concerned with dwelling together in harmony than insisting on our personal preferences.

With that said, there will still be times when two Christians just do not agree on how to proceed in a given situation. That doesn't mean one is right and one is wrong. It just means they don't see eye to eye on everything. When that happens, we don't always have to just tough it out if we have other options.

Such was the case with Paul and Barnabas. Both

Paul and Barnabas were dedicated servants of God. After Paul's conversion, he had a difficult time convincing Christians of his sincerity. And rightly so! Was this not the man who had been a vicious persecutor of Christians? It was Barnabas who persuaded the disciples to give him a chance, and a friendship formed between the two of them (Acts 9:26–28). They even went on a missionary journey together.

Joining them on this journey was Barnabas' cousin, John Mark (Colossians 4:10). For some reason, John Mark decided to return home to Jerusalem while Paul and Barnabas completed the mission (Acts 13:13). John Mark's decision did not sit well with Paul. When another missionary trip was planned, and Barnabas suggested taking John Mark again, Paul balked. A "sharp contention" developed between the two of them (Acts 15:36–41). They couldn't reach an agreement, so they agreed to disagree and split up. Paul took Silas on his journey, while Barnabas went with John Mark.

Here were two servants of God who couldn't agree on an issue. This wasn't a deep theological or doctrinal concern, yet it was a difference of opinion on how to proceed with the work of God. They decided to go their separate ways. We hear nothing about them bad-mouthing each other or putting one another down. They merely agreed to disagree.

The Bible says nothing about who was right or who was wrong in this instance. Some commentaries say Paul was too stubborn. Perhaps, but others feel Paul was guided by logic while warmhearted Barnabas was influenced by John Mark being family. Both Paul and Barnabas were praying to the same God for guidance, and both reached a different conclusion. The point is that in some situations there isn't a right or wrong—just a different point of view.

Although we hear nothing about Paul and Barnabas

working together again, years later Paul mentions Barnabas fondly as a coworker for Christ (1 Corinthians 9:6). It seems Paul and Barnabas maintained mutual respect, which is difficult to do when you agree to disagree with someone. Paul even had a change of heart about John Mark. He said, "Get Mark and bring him with you, for he is useful to me for ministering" (2 Timothy 4:11).

Consider this. Unity in everything will never be achieved unless others agree with everything we say and do or vice versa. However, if we yield to God and let His love guide us, it is possible to dwell together in unity despite disagreements.

Because we all have different strengths and weaknesses, not everyone we meet will like us, nor will we automatically like everyone we meet. And no matter how hard we try, we will not get along with everyone. The sooner we realize that, the better off we'll be. But developing the art of agreeing to disagree can avoid conflict, prevent hasty conclusions, and allow time to reevaluate situations. We don't have to see eye to eye on every issue to live heart to heart.

Suggestions for practicing this choice:

- Practice the art of disagreeing without being disagreeable. Try to focus on what you and another person agree on before discussing what you don't agree upon.
- Do not be judgmental. Give others the benefit of the doubt. As time passes, we may grow to respect and appreciate someone we thought we didn't like.
- Be Christ-centered, not self-centered. Listen to others and try to understand what they mean and where they are coming from.
- Learn to use the phrase "you might be

right" instead of rolling your eyes and saying things like: "Are you out of your mind?"; "You've got to be kidding!"; "That's the stupidest thing I've ever heard!"

- Avoid having a "my way or the highway" attitude. Pray for God to give you a spirit of unity and peace.

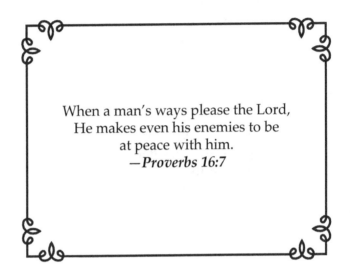

When a man's ways please the Lord,
He makes even his enemies to be
at peace with him.
—*Proverbs 16:7*

Do you have any suggestions for practicing this choice?

1. _____

2. _____

3. _____

4. _____

5. _____

Choice #41
Choose to Fear the Lord

Proverbs has much to say about the fear of the Lord. Proverbs 9:10 tells us, "The fear of the Lord is the beginning of wisdom." What exactly does that mean? Does it mean we tremble with fear every time God's name is mentioned? One dictionary definition of fear is "an unpleasant emotion caused by the belief that someone or something is dangerous, likely to cause pain or a threat."

Does God want us to feel that He is dangerous, a threat, or likely to cause us pain? I don't think so. Although some who don't really know God could interpret it that way. Some live in a constant state of anxiety. They think if they displease God, He will open the trap door to hell. I don't think so. God is love.

However, God does want us to realize He is all-powerful! When we know or recognize God as our Creator and our Master, we have reverence and awe for who He is, what He's done, and what He can do. Awe and reverence is one biblical definition of fear.

If we think of God as a loving Father, we can better relate to this concept. A child has a certain kind of fear or respect for a parent. Children realize parents have power over them. However, if the parents love them and use their power wisely, children know they are loved. There will be consequences for wrong behavior, but children know the motive will be love and what is best for them. Then the children want to please their parents not out of anxiety, but out of love.

The same applies to fearing God. If we have a deep reverence for God and His love for us, we want to please Him—not because we feel frightened if we don't, but because we know it reaps a good result.

If we are aware of God's awesome presence in our lives, we will fear Him in the right way. While it's true that God could cause us pain and misery if we don't obey Him, we don't have to fear His retribution. Although He is all-powerful, He will never misuse that power because God is love (1 John 4:8). We do not need to be frightened of Him. However, we do need to acknowledge His holiness and reverence Him in our lives. We need to honor Him in everything we do. He needs to be our priority and come first in our lives.

Fearing God and giving Him His rightful place in our lives brings blessings:

- Knowledge (Proverbs 1:7)
- Humility (Proverbs 3:7)
- Wisdom (Proverbs 9:10)
- Recognition of evil (Proverbs 8:13)
- Departure from evil (Proverbs 16:6)
- Satisfaction (Proverbs 9:23)
- Prolonged life (Proverbs 10:27)
- Confidence (Proverbs 14:26)
- Spiritual insight (Proverbs 14:27)
- Contentment (Proverbs 15:16)
- Great blessings (Proverbs 22:4)

Consider this. Oswald Chambers had an interesting thought on the fear of God. He said, "The remarkable thing about fearing God is that, when you fear God, you fear nothing else; whereas if you do not fear

God, you fear everything else."[16]

Proverbs 1:7 tells us that the fear of God is the beginning of knowledge. It goes on to say, "But fools despise wisdom and instruction." The choice is simple. Fear God and gain blessings. It would be foolish to do otherwise.

Suggestions for practicing this choice:

- Ask God to help you view Him as a loving God so you can fear Him in the right way.
- Look at creation and realize God is the Creator. This gives you an idea of His awesome power.
- Place importance on the Word of God. Read your Bible and try to apply it in your life. This shows God respect and reverence for what He has to say.
- Think of biblical examples of God's power. He delivered the Hebrew children from the fiery furnace. He shut the mouths of the lions so Daniel would not be eaten. God is all-powerful.
- Realize that fearing God and loving God are not contradictions. We should worship God for who He is, not because we are afraid of Him.

---

[16] Oswald Chambers, *The Highest Good* (Michigan: Discovery House Publishers, 1992).

The fear of the Lord
is the beginning of wisdom.
—*Proverbs 9:10*

Do you have any suggestions for practicing this choice?

1. _____

2. _____

3. _____

4. _____

5. _____

Choice #42
Choose to Overcome Fears

Fear can be a good thing when kept in perspective. For example, fearing God in the right way can bring benefits. God doesn't want us to be afraid of Him, but He does want us to respect His power, acknowledge His holiness, worship His majesty, and reverence Him in our lives. This is not a bad thing. As we continue in a relationship with the living God, we realize He is a God of love and only wants the best for us.

A healthy kind of fear comes with wisdom or heeding caution. It keeps us from jumping off the side of a building thinking we can fly, picking up a rattlesnake thinking we won't get bitten, or driving 150 miles per hour thinking we won't have an accident.

However, some fears paralyze us, keep us from doing what we should or could do, and prevent us from living a fuller, richer life. God wants us to live an abundant life. To do that, we must learn to control unreasonable fears, or else they will control us.

We are a fear-ridden society. Extreme fears result in countless phobias. Just google "phobias" and hundreds will appear. They run the gamut from A to Z. Most of us don't have to deal with the fear of string, infinity, or flutes (Oh yes—those are all phobias!), but we do wrestle with the fear of rejection, hurt, humiliation, abandonment, disappointment, commitment, criticism, loss, the future, and so on. The residual effects of these fears are enough to hold us captive and prevent us from leading the life God intended.

Fear of rejection keeps us from meeting new people. Fear of failure keeps us from accepting responsibility. Fear of looking foolish keeps us from asking questions or trying new things. Fear of the future makes us afraid to enjoy the present. Fear of losing keeps us from playing the game. The list is endless.

God anticipated we would have trouble grappling with these feelings, so He filled the Bible with admonitions to "fear not!" A spirit of fear does not come from God (2 Timothy 1:7). So as we draw closer to God, He calms our fears. When we seek God, He delivers us from our fears (Psalm 34:4). We are not relying on our strength, but God's. When God is with us, He helps and upholds us (Isaiah 41:10).

When we truly realize God is our refuge and strength, we know we have nothing to fear (Psalm 46:1–2). Why be afraid of people when God is our salvation and strength? (Psalm 27:1).

Consider this. God told Joshua not to be afraid or even discouraged because God would be with him wherever he went (Joshua 1:9). God is also with us wherever we go. We are not alone. God says, "Fear not, for I am with you" (Isaiah 41:10). The God of love is with us. God loves us, and there is no fear in love (1 John 4:18–19).

If we make God a priority in our lives, we have nothing to fear. When we seek God, He delivers us from our fears (Psalm 34:4).

Suggestions for practicing this choice:

- Get a handle on fears. Just thinking about them all the time can be instrumental in realizing our fears. We must control our unhealthy fears, not let them control us.
- When you have unwarranted fears, tell yourself over and over again that a spirit of fear does not come from God (2 Timothy 1:7).
- David said that even if he walked through the valley of the shadow of death, he would fear no evil because God was with him (Psalm 23:4–6). When you feel fear coming on, repeat, "God is with me. God is with me. You are with me! You are with me!"
- Seeking God is a key to overcoming fear. However, this seeking of God is not just so He will deliver us from our trials or fears. We seek God so we can place our trust and faith in Him. It's this faith and trust in God that calms our anxious hearts.
- Picture God as a loving father (which He is) who is holding your hand as you walk through life together. He continually whispers, "Fear not! I will help you" (Isaiah 41:13).

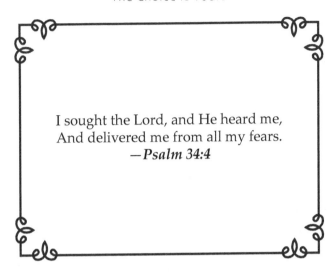

I sought the Lord, and He heard me,
And delivered me from all my fears.
—*Psalm 34:4*

Do you have any suggestions for practicing this choice?

1. _____

2. _____

3. _____

4. _____

5. _____

Choice #43
Choose to Celebrate Life

Some Christians don't seem to be able to smile, laugh, or have a good time. They lack a certain enthusiasm for life. The word *enthusiasm* is derived from the Greek roots *en* meaning "in or within" and *theos*, which means "God." The original meaning was having God within us. Just thinking about God living in us should make us a little enthusiastic. Yet, many Christians are afraid to enjoy life.

It reminds me of the man who had his annual physical check-up, and the doctor told him, "There's no reason why you can't live a completely normal life, as long as you don't enjoy it." We think God says, "There's no reason you can't live a totally committed Christian life, as long as you don't enjoy it."

I think there's some truth in this Billy Sunday quote: "The trouble with many men is that they have got just enough religion to make them miserable."[17] Where does this Christian "downer" attitude come from? Certainly not from God. We miss a lot by keeping God locked in a box of our preconceived ideas of righteousness. Ask yourself the following questions:

Does God like it when we laugh? I think so. Look at creation: elephants with trunks for noses and long-necked giraffes. Way before cartoons, God made Ba-

---

[17] Billy Sunday, *Billy Sunday: The Man and His Message* (Philadelphia: The International Bible House Book and Publishers, authorized edition, 1914), 221.

laam's donkey speak. Why would God tell us a merry heart is good medicine if he didn't want us to be merry? (Proverbs 17:22).

Does Jesus like it when we party? I think so. Jesus's first miracle was turning water into wine at a wedding party (John 2:1–11). We can debate all day long about whether it was wine or grape juice, but the point is it happened at a party, and His intent was to keep that party going. Of course, God is not pleased with drunkenness, lewdness, or vulgarity, but shouldn't we as Christians be able to show the world that people can have a good time without those things?

Does God enjoy our company? I think so. God delights in His people (Psalms 149:4). Delight doesn't mean tolerate; it means He enjoys us.

Does God like dancing? I think so. God turns mourning into dancing (Psalm 30:11). David danced before the Lord with all his might (2 Samuel 6:14).

Does God like it when we shout for joy? I think so. The Psalms are full of Scriptures telling us to do that (Psalm 98:4).

Does God want us to enjoy life? I think so. God provides for our enjoyment (1 Timothy 6:17).

Does God like it when we celebrate? I think so. Every time something good happened in the Bible, there seemed to be some sort of celebration.

When God laid the foundations of the earth, He looked around and said, "It is very good!" Then the morning stars and sons of God shouted for joy (Job 38:7). Sounds like a celebration to me!

For the Old Testament holy days, God told the people to save their money, buy what their hearts desired, share it with others, and rejoice (Deuteronomy 14:26). Sounds like a celebration to me!

After the wall of Jerusalem had been rebuilt, everyone came together to dedicate it to the Lord. There was gladness, thanksgiving, praises to God, plus singing with cymbals, stringed instruments, and harps (Nehemiah 12:27–28). In fact, God had them rejoice with great joy, so much so that "the joy of Jerusalem was heard afar off" (Nehemiah 12:43). Sounds like a celebration to me!

When David and all the house of Israel brought up the ark of the Lord to the city of David, there was much shouting and the sound of the trumpet (2 Samuel 6:14). Sounds like a celebration to me!

There is joy in heaven when one sinner repents (Luke 15:7–10). Sounds like a celebration to me!

If we aren't celebrating and enjoying the Christian life, perhaps we don't know God well enough (Psalm 16:11). In God's presence, there is fullness of joy (Psalm 16:11). I can't help but think that those who live and move and have their being in Christ will be enjoying life (Acts 17:28).

Consider this. God does not take pleasure in joyless Christians leading joyless lives. I'm not saying we should all walk around with fake smiles on our faces pretending to be happy. There are times for quietness and reflection, but God's presence in our lives gives us much to celebrate. God is the eternal joy giver. If we aren't enjoying life, we might not be as close to God as we should be.

Suggestions for practicing this choice:

- Each new day is the day the Lord has made for us to enjoy (Psalm 118:24). So if we wake up breathing, we might want to rejoice!
- Thank God for all your blessings and don't feel guilty for enjoying them.
- Celebrations can help us commemorate our past, appreciate the present, and look forward to the future. There is nothing

wrong with taking a break from our routines to celebrate events.

- Join in the celebration of others. A little card or email message to people on their birthdays, their anniversaries, when they get a promotion, when a baby is born, when a grandbaby is born, when they graduate, and so on can make their day!
- God came so we could have a more abundant life (John 10:10). Why not enjoy it?

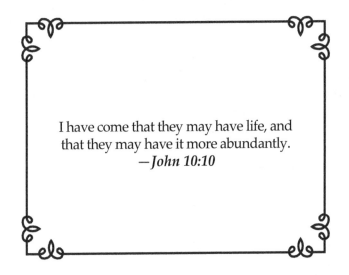

I have come that they may have life, and that they may have it more abundantly.
—*John 10:10*

Do you have any suggestions for practicing this choice?

1. _____

2. _____

3. _____

4. _____

5. _____

Choice #44
Choose to Live without Closure

The psychological use of the word *closure* usually refers to experiencing an emotional conclusion to a difficult life event. Many want to be able to pinpoint this end instead of feeling a sense of ambiguity, so they express the need for closure. This need for closure varies depending on personalities, but for many, not having the closure they think they need prevents them from having peace and moving on.

Unfortunately, we can't always have resolution—at least not the way we want it. Why? Because there are areas of our lives we cannot control. However, we can control whether we allow certain events to hold us captive for the rest of our lives. This makes a real difference in how we live our lives. Do we cope? Do we become bitter or better? Do we move forward?

Here are a few examples of events beyond our control:

- Your twenty-year-old son dies in an unexpected car accident.
- Your mother always favored your brother over you.
- Someone breaks up with you and won't tell you why.
- A friend has a grudge against you and won't tell you what you've done to upset him.

You cannot bring a child back to life and tell them how much you love them once they are gone. To forever live under the guilt of words unspoken keeps you in a world of regret. "If only I had done this" or "if only I hadn't said that" are destructive thoughts because you can't go back and change what's been done. You can, however, determine not to let another day go by without telling a loved one how much you love them.

You cannot make a parent acknowledge their injustice to you if they don't see it. You cannot make someone see what they don't see or don't want to see. After you become a parent, you may decide your parents just did the best they could so you will love them anyway. However, you can be determined not to make the same mistakes with your own children. If your parents were abusive, you might decide to sever your relationship with them.

You cannot force people to love you. If they don't love you, then let them go. Who wants to be in a relationship with someone who doesn't care for you? Decide what you can learn from the situation and move on.

You cannot make people tell you what is bothering them if they refuse to talk to you. If you have apologized for what you've done or what they think you've done, then what more can you do? In the future, choose friends who care as much about how you feel as you care about how they feel.

Closure is not about altering the past. Closure is not about changing others. Closure is not about pretending bad things didn't happen. Closure does not mean something disappears. Closure doesn't mean you block out a painful memory. True closure is about moving on. And in order to move forward, we need to let go of things in our past that would prevent that—things that hold us captive like guilt, regret, unfulfilled expectations, loss, or whatever it is that keeps us thinking we can't be happy unless we get what we want.

Sometimes this kind of closure seems impossible, but with Christ, all things are possible (Matthew 19:26). Paul said he knew he fell short in being the ideal Christian, but through Christ he was able to let go of the past and move toward what God held for him in the future (Philippians 3:1 1–13). We need to press forward.

Consider this. If we are moving forward, we will have to leave some things behind. One of those things may have to be our idea of closure.

Suggestions for practicing this choice:

- Don't think that closure brings peace. Only God can give us peace.
- Don't think that closure will bring happiness. Our happiness cannot be dependent on what others do or don't do.
- It is said that what consumes your mind controls your life. Think about other things and get your mind off the closure you want.
- Do not judge or condemn those who don't give you the closure you want. Pray for them.
- Believe it or not, you can heal and live a productive, Christian life without closure. With God, all things are possible.

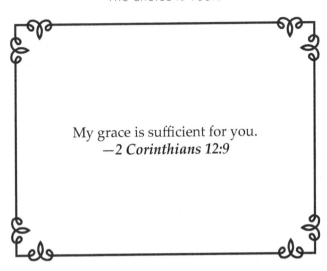

My grace is sufficient for you.
—*2 Corinthians 12:9*

Do you have any suggestions for practicing this choice?

1. _____

2. _____

3. _____

4. _____

5. _____

Choice #45
Choose Not to Worry

People are natural born worrywarts. Did you know that worrywart is an actual word? To my way of thinking, any word with "wart" in it can't be too good. It means one who is inclined to worry unduly. Worry means to have mental distress or agitation from concern for something anticipated. Worry is a big problem. It affects our physical, mental, and spiritual health. Worry can lead to increased heart rate, insomnia, depression, exhaustion, and stress. Worry kills our peace and joy. Worry is a huge waste of time and accomplishes nothing positive.

Yet, we choose to worry. We worry about circumstances we cannot control. We worry about past decisions we cannot alter. We worry about people we cannot change. We worry about what others think of us and worry even more when we discover they haven't been thinking about us at all. Studies show that most of what we worry about never comes to pass.

Jesus knew people were prone to worry, so He asked a rhetorical question to keep worry in perspective. Who can add a single hour to his life or an inch to his stature by worrying? (Matthew 6:27). We all know the answer. No amount of worrying can make us taller or lengthen life. However, it can rob us of sleep, health, and happiness. Worse than that, it can block us from experiencing God's strengthening, healing, and restoration, plus it can steal our confidence and trust in God.

The Bible exhorts us not to worry. Jesus said not to worry about what we will eat, drink, or wear because God knows our needs and will take care of us (Matthew 6:31–32). Paul tells us not to worry about yesterday because it's gone, so look forward to the future (Philippines 3:13). Although we look forward to the future, Jesus said not to worry about it because God has it all under control (Matthew 6:34). This doesn't mean we don't make plans; it just means we don't worry about them. We keep God in our planning process and gladly relinquish our control to Him. We put our trust and confidence in Him—not in ourselves.

We are told not to be anxious about anything (Philippians 4:6). Let not our hearts be troubled (John 14:27). Do not fret (Psalm 37:7). Fretting makes us irritable, irrational, and critical. It's evident in our anxious voice tone. It's reflected in our negative attitudes. It's manifest in our lack of joy. Worrywarts affect not only themselves but those around them.

Worries are like heavy, cumbersome packages we choose to carry. God tells us to cast all our cares on Him. He will carry them for us because He loves us (1 Peter 5:7). God has us carry the light stuff, while He carries the heavy stuff (Matthew 11:30). Worry is heavy stuff. It weighs us down and wears us out. It tires us so much that we don't have time or energy for the things that really matter. What does matter? It's often found amid Scriptures telling us not to worry:

- Do not worry but seek first the kingdom of God (Matthew 6:31–34).
- Don't be anxious. Bring your requests to God in prayer. Give Him thanks. A thankful prayer brings God's peace (Philippians 4:6–7).

- Rest in the Lord. Wait patiently for Him. Do not fret—it only causes harm (Psalm 37:6–7).
- Don't let your heart be troubled. Rejoice (John 14:27–28).

Consider this. Those who are continually seeking God, praying thankfully, resting in the Lord, waiting patiently for Him, and rejoicing don't really have time to worry or fret.

Suggestions for practicing this choice:

- Start your day with prayer and ask God for a positive outlook.
- The moment you start to worry, ask God to calm you, and fill you with His peace.
- Think about this quote from Winston Churchill's book, *Memoirs of the Second World War:* "When I look back on all these worries, I remember the story of the old man who said on his deathbed that he had had a lot of trouble in his life, most of which had never happened."[18]
- Meditate on Scriptures. God tells us to think about things that are just, pure, lovely, of good report, virtuous, and praiseworthy (Philippians 4:8–9).
- I love poetry. Here's a little poem I read years ago. I laminated it to keep in my nightstand. When my mind starts racing at bedtime, I read it over and over to remind me that God can take care of everything.

---

[18] Winston Churchill, AZQuotes.com, Wind and Fly LTD, 2019, https://www.azquotes.com/quote/481788

Tonight my soul be still and sleep
The storms are raging on God's deep
God's deep not thine, be still and sleep
Tonight my soul be still and sleep
God's hand shall still the tempest's sweep
God's hand not thine, be still and sleep
Tonight my soul be still and sleep
God's love be strong while night-hours creep
God's love not thine, be still and sleep
Tonight my soul be still and sleep
God's heaven will comfort those who weep
Gods heaven and thine, be still and sleep
~James Arnold Blaisdell

Which of you by worrying
can add one cubit to his stature?
—*Matthew 6:27*

Do you have any suggestions for practicing this choice?

1. _____

2. _____

3. _____

4. _____

5. _____

Choice #46

Choose to Give Thanks

Legend says that God sent two angels with baskets to earth to gather the prayers of humans. The first angel was to fill a basket with the requests, wants, and desires of people. The other was to gather prayers of thanksgiving. When they returned to God, one angel's basket was heaped high, running over with the countless petitions of men and women. The other angel had searched diligently but alas, returned with an almost empty basket. Are we a thankless society?

Some say we are, especially in the United States. It's hard to be thankful living in a land of plenty. Most of us take for granted having decent food to eat, clean water to drink, shelter from storms, and warm clothing in the winter. Basics? Yes! But these are basics many people live without.

Thanklessness is nothing new. Jesus encountered it during biblical times. Luke 17 gives the account of Jesus stopping outside a village on His way to Jerusalem. There He was met by ten lepers pleading for healing. "Jesus, Master, have mercy on us!" Jesus did have mercy and healed them.

Leprosy was a dreaded, incurable disease that affected the skin, causing disfigurement. The skin would dry up and rot. Fingers, toes, ears, and limbs would waste away and fall off. Lepers lived a life of continuous discomfort and misery. Because the disease was contagious, lepers were not allowed in the city. They were dependent on charity outside the gate or isolated and banished to colonies.

Imagine the gift Jesus gave these lepers by healing them. They were no longer shunned by society. Their lives were restored. Their joy must have been overwhelming. However, only one returned to Jesus to thank Him for what He had done. Jesus noted this ingratitude in Luke 17:17: "Were there not ten cleansed? But where are the nine?"

If people are not thankful for the big things that happen in their lives, it's hard to imagine them being thankful for simple, everyday blessings.

In Old Testament times, being thankful was so important that certain Levites were appointed to give continual praise and thanks to God (1 Chronicles 16:4). Jesus Himself set us an example of thankfulness (Matthew 11:25, 26:7; John 11:41). In all things, we need to be thankful (1 Thessalonians 5:18). That doesn't mean we are thankful when bad things happen. It just means we can always find something to be thankful for regardless of our circumstances. And we need to recognize that blessings come from God (James 1:17).

Consider this. The Bible tells us that those who aren't thankful are foolish (Romans 1:21–22).

When angels in disguise come to fill their baskets at our doors, we shouldn't be afraid to make our requests known to God, but we should do so with thanksgiving (Philippians 4:6). One basket should not outweigh the other in our lives. It is good to give thanks unto the Lord (Psalm 92:1).

Suggestions for practicing this choice:

- Keep a daily gratitude journal.
- If you don't like journaling, keep a running

list of three things you are thankful for each day. Try not to repeat anything.

- Say "thank you" to every person who does something for you. Everyone! Even thank the waiter who takes your order or the guy who bags your groceries. Sure they are getting paid to do it, but a "thank you" from you can make their jobs a little more tolerable.

- Try positive meditation. Each night when you snuggle into bed, don't mentally rehash all the bad things that happened that day, focus on everything that went right—no matter how small. Even in the worst of circumstances, there is always something we can be thankful for.

- For a whole week instead of "gimme, gimme, gimme" prayers, ask God to help you remember all the wonderful things He's done for you in the past and thank Him. One of the sweetest prayers God can hear from your lips is a heartfelt, "Thank You, Lord!"

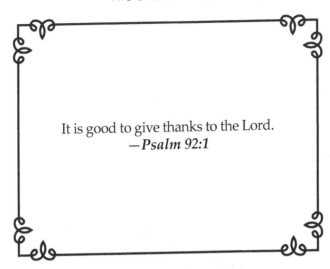

It is good to give thanks to the Lord.
—*Psalm 92:1*

Do you have any suggestions for practicing this choice?

1. _____

2. _____

3. _____

4. _____

5. _____

Choice #47
Choose to Be Balanced

Balance is a part of our daily lives. We want to eat a balanced diet, send our kids to schools with a balanced curriculum, and balance our checkbooks. Balance holds us steady and allows us to cope with life. It keeps us healthy and happy.

Without balance, we tend to go to extremes leading to terrible results. If we eat, eat, eat too many carbs, we get fat. If we work, work, work without rest, we get sick. If we spend, spend, spend without thought, we go bankrupt.

Unfortunately, we all tend to be unbalanced. We think if a little of something is good, then a lot must be better. That is not always true. Prescription drugs, medicinal herbs, or even trace elements might be helpful in moderation, but too much could lead to illness or even death.

Just as there should be a balance in our physical lives, there should be a balance in our Christian lives as well. Zealous Christians don't always understand this and have difficulty seeing the bigger picture.

This was an area of growth for Peter. At first, Peter did not want Christ to wash his feet, until Christ explained, "If I do not wash you, you have no part with me." Then Peter said, "Wash not only my feet but my hands and head, too" (John 13:6–11). I guess he reasoned that if a little washing was good, a lot would be better.

Peter also told Christ he would never deny Him, but he did (Matthew 26:35, 69–75). It's probably best to never say never because we can never be sure we can keep such a promise.

Christ knew Peter didn't fully understand certain things. Peter tended to be an impulsive extremist—and so do we. After Peter grew in grace and knowledge, his statements became more balanced.

Unbalanced Christians go to extremes and miss the mark. For example, some devote their lives to diligent theological study and can debate doctrine with the most learned. However, they may neglect to have an intimate, personal relationship with Jesus and fail to apply Scriptures to their daily lives. Others do just the opposite. They think all they need to do is pray, but they don't study the Bible. So they are swayed by every new idea that comes along (Ephesians 4:14). They don't know what they stand for.

Consider this. Balance does not mean compromising beliefs or being unsure of your faith, nor does it mean shoving spiritual understanding down someone's throat with clever arguments. Balanced Christians know how to combine Bible study with a Christ-centered relationship so they can live life to the fullest. They know how to trust God. They know the Christian life isn't an either-or scenario. They realize we need intellect and emotion, head and heart, form and freedom. Or in the words of Peter, as he matured spiritually, we need grace and knowledge (2 Peter 3:18).

Leading a balanced Christian life is important. Without balance, we fall—physically and spiritually.

Suggestions for practicing this choice:

- The key to keeping good balance is knowing when you've lost it. So take a mental inventory of your life to determine where you are out of balance. There's nothing wrong with a little self-examination (2 Corinthians 13:5).
- Choose one area of your life to work on.
- Decide how you can implement changes to become more balanced in that one area. Develop a plan of action.
- Talk to God about your plan and ask for His help.
- Make Christ the center of your life and balance becomes easier (Matthew 6:33).

But seek first the kingdom of God and His righteousness, and all these things shall be added to you.
—*Matthew 6:33*

Do you have any suggestions for practicing this choice?

1. _____

2. _____

3. _____

4. _____

5. _____

Choice #48
Choose to Make Your Words Sweet

Lawyers who battle it out in court have one goal—to win. Therefore, they do not always play fair. Many times they will ask an objectionable question knowing the judge will not allow it. The judge will strike it from the record and instruct the jury not to give it any credibility when rendering a decision, but it will be too late. Lawyers know the jury will remember what was said. They are counting on it because what is said lingers in a person's mind.

Words have a life of their own. This is why we must be cautious in what we say to others. Even if we apologize for making careless statements, it does not erase the memory of what was said. We cannot strike it from the record or take it back because people will remember it even if we say we didn't really mean it. Spoken words don't just dissolve into the air. They live on, and the damage is done.

No wonder the Bible speaks so much about taming our tongues (James 3:1–12). Both David and James use the metaphor of bridling our tongues (Psalms 39:1; James 1:26). A bridle is a leather harness and bit placed in a horse's mouth to control it. That might seem drastic to us, but in all honesty, some of us could benefit from a built-in muzzle when we are about to say something we are going to regret.

The biblical admonitions about guarding our tongues are plentiful:

- Do not have a flattering tongue (Psalm 5:9).
- Do not have a haughty tongue (Psalm 12:2–4).
- Do not have a lying tongue (Proverbs 25:18).
- Do not have a backbiting tongue (Proverbs 25:23).
- Do not have a talebearer's tongue (Proverbs 18:8).
- Do not have a cursing tongue (Romans 3:13–14).
- Do not have a sharp tongue (Proverbs 12:18).
- Do not have a gossiping tongue (Romans 1:29).

Perhaps the hardest tongue to guard against is one that manifests itself when we least expect it. Unfortunately, this seems to happen with those who are closest to us. We say something stupid or hurtful, and we don't even know why. We might think, "I wonder where that came from?" But the heart knows (Matthew 12:34). Someone or something can trigger unresolved issues within us, and we end up regurgitating them on others.

Solomon said to weigh our words carefully (Ecclesiastes 5:2–3). James said to think before we speak (James 1:19). Jesus said what goes into our mouths is not as important as what comes out (Matthew 15:11).

Proverbs 16:24 tells us what should come out of our mouths. "Pleasant words are like a honeycomb, sweetness to the soul, and health to the bones." We should speak loving words. Gracious words. Caring words. Pleasant words. These words are sweet to our souls and possess healing power, making us happier and healthier. They are good spiritually and physically.

Using an analogy about honey with words is pure genius. Honey not only tastes sweet, but it has health benefits as well. From ancient times, honey was used as a food and as medicine. Ancient Egyptians made offerings of honey to their gods. Honey is an all-natural, high-energy food loaded with antioxidants. It's used to help suppress coughs and reduce allergy symptoms. Perhaps the most amazing fact about honey is that it's a natural antibiotic. When applied to a burn or wound, it promotes healing because of its antibacterial and anti-inflammatory effects.

No wonder honey is used as an analogy for using our words like a honeycomb—sweet to the soul and healing to the bones. Here are some effects of using words for the good of others:

- A wise tongue promotes healing (Proverbs 12:18).
- Good words make a heart glad (Proverbs 12:25).
- A soothing tongue is like the tree of life (Proverbs 14:4).
- Words of edification impart grace to hearts (Ephesians 4:29; 1 Thessalonians 5:11).

Consider this. Heartfelt words spoken with kindness, consideration, and love are beautiful (Proverbs 25:11). They can calm, cheer, and encourage others (Proverbs 12:25). However, careless, thoughtless words can be poisonous (James 3:8).

Every time you speak, remember that words have a life of their own. What you say today lives on tomorrow. If we make our words sweet, they will be much easier to eat—if we must!

Suggestions for practicing this choice:

- Don't be too quick to respond. A moment of thought or a little hesitation might improve what you want to say immensely.
- If you are discussing a delicate situation, say a little mental prayer before you respond. "Lord, what should I say? Please guide my words. Please put Your words in my mouth."
- If you are thinking you probably shouldn't say something, then don't say it. A good clue is when you say, "I probably shouldn't say this but . . ."
- Don't pretend to know what you are talking about when you don't. And don't assume you know what you are talking about.
- I know you've seen this acronym before, but it's a good one. Think before you speak.

> **T** — Is it true?
> **H** — Is it helpful?
> **I** — Is it inspiring?
> **N** — Is it necessary?
> **K** — Is it kind?

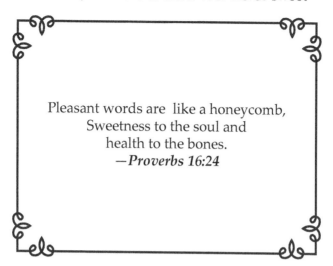

Pleasant words are like a honeycomb,
Sweetness to the soul and
health to the bones.
—*Proverbs 16:24*

Do you have any suggestions for this choice?

1. _____

2. _____

3. _____

4. _____

5. _____

Choice #49

Choose to Look to God, Not People

One of my favorite biblical images is in the book of Daniel. The king had a dream. He envisioned a great idol with a head of gold, arms of silver, a belly and thighs of brass, and legs of iron. It was a stately image with the strength of metals and ores. However, this seemingly strong idol had feet made of part iron and part clay. Therefore, when a stone smote the image at this most vulnerable part, it broke into pieces, and the idol fell. You see, dried clay is easily fragmented when hit just the right way (Daniel 2:31–36).

I think this dream holds a life lesson for all of us. God is not an idol; He's the real thing. His feet are not made of clay. When we look to Him, we will never be misled or disappointed.

However, many of us tend to look to other people instead of God. We make idols of people, forgetting all humans have clay feet. No matter how wonderful we think people are, they will eventually disappoint us. It can happen with those we love like a mother, father, sister, brother, mate, child, or friend. It can happen with those we set up as authority figures, those we admire, we mentor, or who mentor us. People are human.

Those we are closest to or look up to the most have the greatest ability to hurt or disappoint us. It may happen in a tone of voice we don't like or a comment that hits us the wrong way. Or maybe they just flat out make a big mistake, and it doesn't matter how much they apologize, we just can't forgive. All people are human and have clay feet. And when that rock of offense hits those clay feet, the wonderful image we have of a person comes tumbling down.

We focus on Scriptures that say it would be better to drown than offend one of God's little ones and those telling us not to deliberately offend (Matthew 18:6; 1 Corinthians 8:13). Good stuff! However, sometimes, we need to focus on Scriptures telling us that nothing will offend those who love God. They have great peace (Psalm 119:165).

Most of us are not the "little ones" in Christ. We've been around awhile. We might even be considered the "old-timers" who should be spiritually mature. We shouldn't be getting offended. We shouldn't be imputing wrong motives. We shouldn't be over-evaluating every statement people make. We need to be looking to God, not people.

People are flawed. Even heroes of the faith were imperfect. One day Moses was parting the Red Sea, and another day he was striking the rock out of anger. One day Elijah was calling fire down from heaven, and another day he was hiding in a cave afraid of Jezebel. One day David was killing Goliath with a slingshot, and another day he was trying to justify having an affair with Bathsheba.

Why? Because they were human. And therein lies the problem if we try to make idols out of Christian leaders, or friends, or relatives, or anyone. They are all human. They will eventually disappoint us.

Paul knew he could make mistakes. He could disappoint. He even disappointed himself with his own humanness (Romans 7:18–21). That's why he said to follow him as he followed Christ (1 Corinthians 11:1). Jesus Christ never makes mistakes. Jesus Christ does not have clay feet.

Consider this. To have peace, we must look to God foremost. Then we must look for the good in those who strive to serve and obey Him.

Suggestions for practicing this choice:

- Since we are all human, let's cut each other a little slack. Accept that apology. Overlook that comment. Maybe it wasn't their tone of voice that was off but our hearing. Maybe they didn't even say what we thought they said.
- Try not to be so touchy and take everything personally.
- Try to give others the benefit of the doubt.
- Don't be judgmental. God will deal with people in His way and in His time.
- Realize that most people are just trying to do the best they can and follow God to the best of their ability. They are human—just like you!

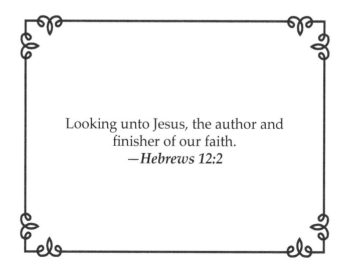

Looking unto Jesus, the author and
finisher of our faith.
—*Hebrews 12:2*

Do you have any suggestions for practicing this choice?

1. _____

2. _____

3. _____

4. _____

5. _____

Choice #50

Choose to Recognize a Miracle

In his book, *My Utmost for His Highest,* Oswald Chambers said, "We look for visions from heaven and for earth-shaking events to see God's power. . . . One of the most amazing revelations of God comes to us when we learn that it is in the everyday things of life that we realize the magnificent deity of Jesus Christ."[19]

Unfortunately, people don't want to see the miracles in everyday life. They want to experience a faith healing or spectacular event before they will believe in God's existence. This philosophy can be dangerous because not all supernatural happenings come from God.

- Deuteronomy 13:1–3 says to beware of those who foretell dreams or signs and wonders that come to pass, then encourage you to follow other gods than the one true God. So others, besides God, can perform certain signs and wonders.
- Mark 13:22–23 tells us to be on guard because some can perform miracles that can deceive us into thinking they represent Christ.
- Matthew 7:22–23 tells us that many will

---

[19] Oswald Chambers, *My Utmost for His Highest* (Michigan: Discovery House Publishers, 1992).

come to God, pointing out that they had performed miracles, but God will say, "I never knew you. Get away, you evildoers!"

- 2 Thessalonians 2:8–9 reminds us that Satan has the power to perform counterfeit miracles, signs, and wonders.
- Exodus 7:11 recounts how Moses and Aaron performed miracles such as having a staff turn into a snake, but Pharaoh summoned his sorcerers, and they did the same thing.

Sometimes God provides supernatural happenings, and sometimes He doesn't. In Christ's hometown of Galilee, Christ didn't do many miracles because of their lack of faith (Matthew 13:58). Was this because Christ's miracles are dependent on our faith? Not at all! But this was Christ's hometown where people knew Him, so what would have been the point of doing a lot of miracles? They wouldn't have believed anyway, because contrary to popular opinion, miracles do not increase belief. The Israelites proved that. God performed miracle after miracle for them, including parting the Red Sea, and they still didn't believe He could take care of them in the Promised Land.

The need for Christ to authenticate His message through miracles has long passed. His message speaks for itself. Sadly, some professing Christians are still seeking signs and wonders long after their conversion. This is not so much that they doubt Christ's existence as they are looking for a high that comes from the miracle. But when we are always looking for the next big thrill in our lives to feel God's presence, we forget that He has been with us all along. We miss the daily walk. We miss what is right in front of our eyes.

Consider this. In biblical times, many missed the miracle of Christ's birth because they were looking for another kind of miracle—a Messiah descending from heaven with a flaming sword of righteousness to deliver them from oppressive Roman rule. They did not recognize the Christ child in the manger as their Savior. They missed what was right before their eyes.

Do we see God in our everyday lives? Do we see God when the six o'clock alarm rings, when we take a shower, brush our teeth, carpool the kids, drive to work in the same old car to the same old job and come home to the same old family, then cook something to eat, do the dishes, help with homework, and fall into bed dog-tired? Can we cheerfully get up the next day, do it all again, and stay totally centered on God? That's a miracle.

Healthy Christians can go through life without God having to supernaturally zap them with addictive spiritual methamphetamine to get them through the day. As we grow in God's grace, we realize the miracle of God revealing Himself to us all the time. It might be in the laughter of a child, the smile of a coworker, clouds in the sky, sunlight on a window pane, or a flower garden.

Do we realize that life itself is a miracle? The whole universe is one miracle after another—not chance happenings but actual miracles! If we are truly looking for a miracle, we need look no further than where we are. For where we are, God will be. He'll never leave us or forsake us, no matter what. If we don't see that as a miracle, there is no need to look anywhere else because we'll never find it.

Suggestions for practicing this choice:

Ask God to help you see the miracles around you in everyday life. Thinking about these quotes will help:

- "The invariable mark of wisdom is to see the miracle in the common."[20]
  —Ralph Waldo Emerson
- "There are only two ways to live your life. One is as though nothing is a miracle. The other is as if everything is."[21]
  —Albert Einstein
- "Miracles come in moments. Be ready and willing."[22]
  —Wayne Dyer
- "The visible world is a daily miracle for those who have eyes and ears."[23]
  —Edith Wharton
- "Miracles surround us at every turn if we but sharpen our perception of them." [24]
  —Willa Cather

---

[20] Ralph Waldo Emerson Quotes. BrainyQuote.com, BrainyMedia Inc, 2019. https://www.brainyquote.com/quotes/ralph_waldo_emerson_125383

[21] Albert Einstein, Quotes. BrainyQuote.com, BrainyMedia Inc, 2019, https://www.brainyquote.com/quotes/albert_einstein_390808

[22] Wayne Dyer Quotes, BrainyQuote.com, BrainyMedia Inc, 2019, https://www.brainyquote.com/quotes/wayne_dyer_165697.

[23] Edith Wharton, AZQuotes.com, Wind and Fly LTD, 2019, https://www.azquotes.com/quote/86755

[24] Willa Cather, AZQuotes.com, Wind and Fly LTD, 2019, https://www.azquotes.com/quote/927196

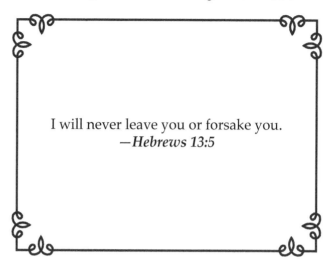

I will never leave you or forsake you.
—*Hebrews 13:5*

Do you have any suggestions for practicing this choice?

1. _____

2. _____

3. _____

4. _____

5. _____

Choice #51
Choose to Shine a Light

When I think about the birth of Christ, I think of light. A star shone bright, casting light to guide the wise men to where Christ was born. Jesus, Himself, will later tell us, "I have come into the world as a Light, so that no one who believes in me should stay in darkness" (John 12:46).

Scripture often refers to Jesus as the Light. Jesus, the Light, came to the world, but men loved darkness instead of the Light (John 3:19–21). As Christians, we should love the Light, not darkness.

Light and dark often serve as metaphors in the Bible to contrast good and evil. With so much evil and darkness in the world, it's easy for us to get discouraged. Yet, most would agree that it is "better to light a candle than curse the darkness."

That familiar saying was first spoken in public in 1961 by Peter Benenson, the British lawyer who founded Amnesty International. A candle encircled with barbed wire became the society's emblem. Paul said something similar when he told us to "cast off the works of darkness and put on the armor of light." He goes on to reveal what this armor of light is: "Put on the Lord, Jesus Christ" (Romans 13:12–14).

Jesus living His life in us makes us a light in the world as well. Our lights should not be hidden. People don't light a lamp and put it under a bowl so no one can see it. Instead, they put it on a stand so it will give light to everyone in the house. We are encouraged to let our lights shine before others, that they may see our good deeds which glorify our Father in heaven (Matthew 5:14–16).

Never underestimate the ability of your light to influence the world for good. Impacting just one person with the light of Christ can make a difference. Unfortunately, many would rather curse the darkness than shine their lights. Some would prefer to condemn others rather than share God's love and grace.

Similarly, we should never let the darkness in the world keep us from shining a light, no matter how small we may think it is. Jesus tells us that darkness cannot overcome the light (John 1:5). Although we might feel like a small candle in vast darkness, even a small candle can benefit others. It offers light and warmth. Even the small ways we reflect the light of Jesus through love and kindness can benefit others.

We are God's children—children of Light (1 Thessalonians 5:5). Everything we do can bring light to others (Colossians 4:5–6). Being a good example shines a light. The testimony we share but not force on others shines a light. The Scripture we quote shines a light. The encouragement we give shines a light. The love we show others shines a light. We are told to let our light shine before others (Matthew 5:16).

Consider this. Sometimes we forget that we were all once in darkness, needing light. Now we are children of Light (Ephesians 5:8). This would not have been possible without the birth of Christ—the Light coming into the world.

Suggestions for practicing this choice:

- Think about this quote from William Shakespeare: "How far that little candle throws his beams! So shines a good deed in a weary world."[25]
- Stop focusing on yourself and focus on others. What you do for others, you are doing for Christ (Matthew 25:45).
- Force yourself to smile at everyone you meet. Smiles are a universal language. Not only do smiles lift spirits, but they are also contagious. Statistics show that a person who is given a smile will more than likely give one to someone else.
- Did you know that light travels faster than sound? So learn to speak less and shine more!
- Here are some ways to let the light of Christ shine through you: encourage others, learn to laugh, forgive, be patient, be kind—you get the idea. Reflect Jesus Christ!

---

[25] William Shakespeare Quotes, BrainyQuote.com, BrainyMedia Inc, 2019, https://www.brainyquote.com/quotes/william_shakespeare_155088

Let your light so shine before men,
that they may see your good works
and glorify your Father in heaven.
—*Matthew 5:16*

Do you have any suggestions for practicing this choice?

1. _____

2. _____

3. _____

4. _____

5. _____

Choice #52
Choose to Keep Moving Forward

I'm a big believer in living in the present. So many people live in the past, constantly lamenting what might have been. They obsess over things like: If only I had married the geek I thought was a loser in college who became a millionaire. If only I had taken that job with the start-up company that I thought would go nowhere but went sky-high. If only I hadn't gotten pregnant at sixteen. If only I had finished college instead of dropping out. If only I hadn't gotten drunk and had a tattoo of a naked lady put on my arm. If only, if only, if only . . .

Everyone's life is full of missed opportunities, some unwise decisions, and regret. These things cannot be changed. Yet many seem held captive by things they can do nothing about.

Others put their lives on hold, waiting for the future. As soon as all their preconceived needs are met, they will get their priorities straight and live the good life.

Both extremes of living in the past or waiting for the future are immobilizing and prevent us from going forward. Christian lives should not be held in suspended animation. We must keep moving by walking with God on our day by day journey. That's what living in the present is all about.

God knows all our needs and doesn't want us to worry about them (Matthew 6:25–32). He is fully capable of taking care of them. Our focus needs to be on seeking the kingdom of God (Matthew 6:33–34). This means participating in a relationship with God daily. Seek Him day by day. That's our priority—and we can't do it when we are constantly lamenting the past or waiting for the future.

When we learn to do this, we don't have to wait for the future. We can look forward and move into the future. Living in the present by walking daily with God helps us accept and learn from our past, then move into the future. We are moving toward something. Paul says to forget what is behind and move forward (Philippians 3:13–14).

Christians cannot afford to be stagnant. We need to learn from the past, so we don't make the same mistakes repeatedly. Live in the present to continue enjoying a lasting relationship with God but move forward with Him into the future.

Consider this. We don't know what lies ahead of us, but we do know our God has it all under control. He goes before us. He walks beside us. Our days are in His loving hands (Psalm 31:15). We can move forward with confidence in Him. It beats being left behind.

Suggestions for practicing this choice:

- When you are tempted to lament the past, think of what happened to Lot's wife when she looked back (Genesis 19:26).
- Focus on your strengths, not your weaknesses. Look for ways you can serve others using the gifts and talents God has given you.
- Focus on how far you have come, not how far you have to go. Sometimes it's a positive reinforcement to list what you have done. There will always be stuff left to do.

- Stay close to God. Walk with Him. Talk to Him. That's how a relationship is sustained.
- Work on self-improvement. That's what New Year's resolutions are all about. But instead of resolving to lose weight, which will only last until you start craving potato chips or chocolate cake, why not focus on being a nicer person? Choose to smile, do some random acts of kindness, or say "please" and "thank you." You'll be happier, and so will everyone around you.

. . . forgetting those things which are behind and reaching forward to those things which are ahead.
—*Philippians 3:13*

Do you have any suggestions for practicing this choice?

1. _____

2. _____

3. _____

4. _____

5. _____

Order Information

REDEMPTION
P R E S S

To order additional copies of this book, please visit
www.redemption-press.com
or by calling toll-free 1-844-2REDEEM.

CPSIA information can be obtained
at www.ICGtesting.com
Printed in the USA
LVHW090429141020
668770LV00001B/392